G000041353

A BOY FROM
PRIMROSE HILL

BY

JEREMY GOODCHILD

ISBN: 9781687137685 (paperback)

For Colin
Jonothan, Sophie and Freddie
with my love
and in memory of
Terrie Varley and Tracy Davenport

CHAPTER'S

1

PRIMROSE HILL

Known locally as the 'Island' as it was slap bang in the middle of surrounding St John's Wood, Camden Town, Chalk Farm and Hampstead, Primrose hill in Regents Park London NW1 in the 1960's was a very pleasant part of central London. (It still is) The steep hill which was our playground as children was built its rumoured by burying thousands of dead bodies after the great plague of London on top of each other.

The top of the hill is flat with spectacular views all over London. It also served as a defence area during world war two. There were two enormous guns stationed on the top of it nicknamed "big Bertha's" which were there to try and shoot down German planes flying over London to bomb it, making everyone in the vicinities windows cave in when they were fired.

Our house was positioned just behind it. The view from our kitchen was overlooking the Aviary at London Zoo and eventually the GPO tower.

Everybody knew everybody in those days. My own family of local relatives numbered into the 30's. I entered this world rather late on weds 6th of July 1960. I was delivered at home at number 6 Chamberlain Street just of Regents Park Road. The second child of Don and Diane Goodchild the other sibling being older sister Deborah.

It was a friendly local community made up of all sorts of characters. There were always a large number of actors and theatre folk and writers in the area, due to its close proximity to the theatres of the West End. Lots of local people of course and a few Italians, Polish, Greek and Irish. So it was always fairly cosmopolitan we all lived happily together long before anyone had ever heard of being in the EU.

Chamberlain Street is a small cul de sac just off of Regents Park Road shopping area and as children we used to play out in the street as it was perfectly safe to. We were a colourful mix.

The houses were fairly large covering 4 floors plus attics. These were inevitably split up into apartments. Indeed we occupied two floors with my grandparents Sid and Kathleen living in the basement flat.

There were Lodgers on the top floor. Camden council hadn't then given out modernisation grants. Although we were considered lucky to have an indoor toilet, we didn't have a bathroom and had to use a big tin tub in the kitchen. Now when you tell younger people this they recoil in horror, but it was just normal then, everybody in the area lived the same way. We didn't feel deprived because we were not.

My Father was a lapsed Catholic born in Larne in Northern Ireland. My great grandmother was a mid-wife in Larne, so when my grandmother (a nurse) fell pregnant she flew home for her mother Jessica Mc'Claverty to deliver the children including two other Boys, Harry the eldest and Leslie the youngest.

My Father Thomas (always known as Don) after volunteering for the R.A.F towards the end of the war, worked at Curry and Paxton's in Camden Town. Here he served his apprenticeship and became a successful optical engineer designing lenses for cameras and spectacles. He served them loyally for 25 years until the company relocated to Corby. I only mention him being a Catholic because my mother was a Protestant and in those days, it caused slight outrage.

My grandmother Kathleen who lived in the basement was a devout Catholic and went to mass three times a day if she could. When my parents married she refused to go into the Protestant church to watch the service but joined in for the pictures outside! However she was a gentle soul who was a loyal nurse for years. Her family in Larne were all linked to the medical world or the Navy, They were originally from Strathclyde in Scotland. My father had nasty memories from attending a boys Catholic school in Haverstock hill, and didn't have a good word to say about Nuns and Monks so I was never baptised, something I am grateful for.

His father Sid was a lovely quiet gentle man who had been gassed in the First World War. He had lost all of his hair and wore the most dreadful toupee, probably Government Issue. He was a terrific pianist. He didn't follow the family business, they were Butchers based in Mornington Crescent in North London. His job was working for a famous DIY man called Barry Bucknell. Barry was very famous in the 1960's, he had his own TV show on the BBC called "Do it yourself" it had 6 million viewers and was the first ever makeover show on TV. Although the programmes went out live Barry was really just a TV presenter and not much good at DIY. My grandfather Sid did all the preparation work behind the scenes, the carpentry etc. The Bucknell's had a factory in Camden Town.

My mother Diane came from a large family called Major. The Majors were quite well known locally and lived at No 7 Berkley road also off of Regents Park Road. My grandfather John was a greengrocer, a very good one. He had three shops at one time. Two in St John's wood and one in Regents Pk Road. He'd worked hard all his life. He started as a young boy as a Costermonger (a market seller) selling bananas on Waterloo bridge from the age of 7. A Cockney boy his mother a local money lender and greengrocer taught him well about hard work and business. The shop in St John's Wood high street was a big success, because he went to Covent Garden market everyday at 3-4 am and bought the best. He was known to everyone at Covent Garden by the nickname of 'Brownie' although no one can remember why except something to do with Hovis bread. His clientele consisted of locals, well heeled Jewish housewives who lived in St John's wood queuing up in their chauffeur driven cars while handing out their orders from the window. They knew he would only supply quality goods. He was the first greengrocer in London to stock Avocados and he was head hunted by Fortnum and Masons to be their head buyer, he refused.

It also became a bit of a hangout for local out of work actors. At the back of the shop my grandmother Irene always had a big pot of soup or stew on the go, and she would feed them all. It became known as the 'Day and Night club' nicknamed by the actress and singer Frances Day. Some of them went on to become big stars and remembered the Majors generosity, giving them free tickets for shows they were in, or welcomed them to the Players Theatre under the arches at Charing Cross. All this ended in 1960 the year I was born as my grandfather Major thought he had cancer. He sold up the business and retired. The good news was he didn't have cancer. Men of his generation and background didn't believe in doctors, and you only went into hospital to die.

Back, Doug, Jan middle Bertha Nellie pat Renee
Mace, front Roderick Andrew Barry

A young Kathleen aged
18 Grandmother

Bertha Nellie and
Granny pickett

Colin Teddy
Tony and Pat

Grandad Go both grans Ronnie in front and Colin in braces

Grandad Syd Goodchild

Great Granny Pickett of the Round house.

Irene Major Grandmother

Kathleen Nana Goodchild

Mum aged 16

Nanny goodchild young girl

2

AN IDYLLIC CHILDHOOD

My first memory is of being in a pram being pushed up the road with my mother and her sister Pat. They stopped at a record store probably in Camden Town and bought a selection of the latest 45's. They handed me one called 'My Mothers Eyes' by a singer called Ricky Stevens. I still have it and still play it now in 2019!

Music is a very important part of my life, my grandmother Irene was renowned for her Christmas parties. The front door at number 7 Berkeley road was open to everyone Christmas night and after the pub (The Chalk farm Tavern) closed; everyone would come back to the house for a party. There would always be plenty of food and drink especially seafood. Jellied eels, whelks, winkles, prawns and of course ham and turkey and plenty of salad.

There was a piano in the upstairs parlour and this particular year there was no pianist. This was usually my other grandfather Sid who was a really good piano player, especially boogie woogie. From the age of three I was able to pick out a few notes on the piano, I could always play by ear and I duly managed 'knees up mother brown' after my grandmother sang a few bars, not a song she liked but it got the adults going. That was the first thing I ever played on the piano and would stand me in good stead years later. I got a big round of applause and that year the floor didn't cave in as it had done in previous years. I loved those parties.

Playing in the street wasn't really necessary (although we did) as we had Primrose hill on the doorstep. We spent most days in the spring and summer there looking for conkers and acorns, playing on the swings and daring each other to hang off the roundabouts. These were circular and held about eight people and someone used to whiz them around at break neck speed as you tried to hold on. Health and safety tsars today would have breakdowns. My cousin Suzanne Goodchild would often be with us, my sister's age, her mother's family the Aylett's owned the local pub The Chalk Farm Tavern (now the Lemonia Greek restaurant) in Regents Park Road where they all used to socialise.

One of the delights of living in Primrose hill was when it snowed in the winter we would dig out our sledges and sleighs and drag them over to the hill. Climbing right to the top we would take it in turns to race to the bottom. If Auntie Pat could be persuaded to come, it caused us much mirth as she was a large lady. We'd wait until she lowered herself onto the sledge and before she could sit we'd kick it away under her causing her to collapse in the snow. I can remember rolling around in the snow in hysterics laughing at this, crying with laughter while she cursed us (she could make a sailor blush!)

Like most kids we played hopscotch, skipping, ball games, marbles and another favourite, 'knock down ginger' Knocking on doors and running away.

A certain Cilla Black was a regular victim of our childish pranks. She was just becoming famous then and had moved into a mews house off of Regents Park Road. Poor Cilla, she was very shy in those days and used to go bright red if approached for an autograph. She was number one in the charts at the time with 'Anyone who had a heart' it was a huge hit. I remember one Irish Family who lived in our street called the Harte's who loved this song. They would play it on their record player and leave the holding arm off so that the record arm would continually go back onto the record over and over again. It must have been summer, because they had the windows wide open and deafened us all for hours on end with "our Cilla".

Our local sweet shop and newsagents 'Sparks' was where we used to go for all those lovely old fashioned sweets like sherbet dip and pear drops. There was a tub in the corner where for a few pennies you could put your hand in amongst the straw and take a lucky dip for a prize. The owner wasn't too pleased if you got a good one.

Ruby Sparks the owner was a reformed gangster and a surly man. He got his name because as a young burglar he had robbed a Mayfair mansion and stole 45 thousand pounds worth of rubies belonging to a Maharajah. He didn't believe they were real so he gave them all away. He then formed a Bonnie and Clyde style team with a woman called Lillian Goldstein to operate London's first smash and Grab crime business with Lillian as the getaway driver. Shame Ruby never had a few baubles left to put in the lucky dip.

Our neighbours were a very eclectic mix. Opposite to us in Chamberlain Street lived the Italian Bravatti family. Tina Bravatti gave us our first taste of Pasta Shuta the Italian dish which is like tagliatelle with Bolognese sauce.

Her Brothers used to make their own wine. They would tread it in bare feet inside big barrels in the basement of the house. As children we used to queue up outside the Airy steps (the entrance to the basement) and the men would hand us out glasses of pure grape juice to drink before it was turned into wine. I love this memory.

We had Mr Joplin a solicitor who drove a vintage Bentley with a big step up board to get into it. We used to drive him mad jumping on and off of it. Next door were a professional family called the Marriott's, they became good friends. Jenny and Phillip Were also solicitors and they had two daughters called Victoria and Sophia who were my main playmates. They were well off because the girls always had a nanny. We would spend hours in the garden (back yards) practicing doing the Twist. A dance craze sweeping the world. I was always obsessed with records and I had two wind up gramophones we used to play the records on in the garden. Our 1960's version of the Wireless speaker I suppose.

Jenny and Phillip I remember didn't believe in television. They considered it to low brow I think. They did relent though on one occasion when they and several others piled into our sitting room to watch live the funeral of Winston Churchill. Jenny gave me an early introduction to classical music by kindly buying me a copy of Mozart's Eine kleine nacht music to listen to. She was probably sick off Chubby Checker by then. I was also given a box set of the Opera Carmen by friends Marion and Zenon, Polish hairdressers with a shop in Regents park road. They used to let me go up to their flat and play their record collection on their radiogram.

My mother Diane and her sister Pat were also very keen on opera and the classics so I had a wide range of musical influences at an early age. I knew Borodins Polovtsian dances by heart by the age of six. They both liked to play the piano too. So with my ability to play by ear, I was sent off to a music teacher in St Georges terrace for an appraisal. I was aged about 4 years old. He declared I had perfect pitch and took me on as a student to teach me the piano. My dear friend Dolly Prior who had 'Palmers' greengrocers in Regents Park Road remembers to this day me trotting past the shop at that age with my music case under my arm. Dolly and her late Husband Wally have remained friends of ours to this day and I grew up with her children Lesley, Karen and Jane. They had a brother Derek also. They were the reason we ended up living in Sussex eventually.

My Mother also enrolled me into the young music makers group at Hampstead where I was going to learn the guitar, but I didn't take to this for some reason. At school I was always in the choirs and music groups.

Around this time I remember being called out from the back yard to go upstairs to meet some people. I had an ability to identify the titles of records without being able to read and write yet, even from a distance. Somehow a journalist from the Sunday Mirror heard about this "phenomena" (probably one of our neighbours) and came around to interview me and take pictures which later appeared in the paper.

Next I was in a film. Again one of our neighbours probably one of the Gloucester Terrace brigade was a film maker and made a short film of first, a chipmunks tea party over in Regents Park Zoo and then a tea party with Me, Karen and Jane Prior and a few other children doing the same spliced together. Not sure what the point was and I don't think it won any awards but it did appear on the BBC one night before the 6 o'clock news, much to our delight.

School was Primrose hill school in Princess Road where my sister went and my mother and her siblings before me. I started in nursery school and then went on to Primary school. A bleak looking Victorian building it was a great school with very good teachers. Mine was a Miss Gibson whom I adored and she me. When I left she wrote to me for some time. I still have one of the letters. You always remember good teachers.

Sundays was the only day in the week we had time to spend quality time with my father. He took my sister Deborah and I out every Sunday over to Regents Park which you access by walking through Primrose hill. We both have wonderful memories of this. In the good weather he would take us rowing on Regents Park Lake, mooring at this little central island we used to think was magic, with three stones that we used to climb over and make a wish.

On the way back we would listen to 'Family Favourites' on a transistor radio and wander around the outside of London Zoo looking at the animals and sucking on merry maid chocolate éclair toffees and aniseed twists. Then home for Sunday lunch, bliss.

My father worked 6 days a week then plus overtime. So the only time we saw him was when he came home from work. We would be tucked up in bed by 6 pm where my father would come in and read us a story. Usually our favourite Brer Rabbit by Enid Blyton so Sundays were special for us.

Our annual holidays were spent at first in Cliftonville near Margate and then Shanklin in the Isle of White, where we would meet up with the same families every year for swimming and beach games on the sand. Shanklin beach cafe made the best Cornish pasties I've ever tasted, and after swimming all day and playing bat and ball we were always starving and couldn't wait for one of these they were delicious. My mother would always have a picnic hamper stuffed with food and drinks as well. We had all given up on the crisps with the little bag of salt in the blue paper and embraced the new cheese and onion flavour with relish. There were only two flavours then.

I remember my father always carrying all of the suitcases and us walking behind. We would always walk to the tube station to get to Victoria or wherever. We never thought of getting taxis. There were no minicabs then and no black cabs passed the door and we were not on a bus route in either Primrose hill or later Edgware. In Edgware it was about a mile to the nearest tube from our house, so my poor father's arms must have ached, but he never complained, just whistled away happily.

Lots of the rest of my spare time would have been at my grandmother Majors house, where I could practice the piano and also play her collection of Al Jolson Max Miller and Vera Lynn 78's. (Records)

My grandmother Major, my mother and her sister Pat were very influential people in my early years. Three very strong women with a great sense of humour. Grandmother Major was born in Kettleburgh in Suffolk. They later moved to Sweffling. She was the eldest of three sisters with Bertha and Ellen (Nellie) the youngest. She also had three brothers Tom Owen and Brian. She trained to be a Sunday school teacher and had decided to become a full time teacher, but the first world war put a stop to that and the "Lady of the Manor" When she told the titled lady her plans to become a teacher she dismissed these ambitions as foolish and said you must get to work straight away and earn money to help your poor mother.

My great grandfather Mace Pickett had gone off to fight and there was little money coming in. So at aged 14 she was sent off to work in service at a big local house belonging to some lord or other. From humble beginnings she eventually became a great cook.

Her father Mace Pickett was a great big man, He worked as a Drayman, but when he was younger his family were traveling showman and Mace was a bare knuckle fighter and he boxed in the ring with kangaroos at travelling fairs. In that era big men often fought poor kangaroos in rings for money, although he was a gentle giant in reality and wouldn't hurt a fly. His mother was a wonderful woman known to all as Granny of the roundhouse. (because she lived in a round house in Sweffling Suffolk) She was an early feminist in the fact she was an entrepreneur. She was what was called a "tally woman" She bought stock wholesale from suppliers then sold it to the community for a profit. She would go around the streets on a horse and cart and charge people so much a week for household items. An early form of credit. Maces father Pickett got killed in the boar war and granny remarried a man called Smith and went on to have a further 8 children I believe. They had wonderful names like Nicodemus, Kenza, Adolphus,Venus and Ethelia. A strong woman obviously.

There was always a rumour of a Gypsy connection in our family but it seems they were showman on that side not Gypsy but maybe it had something to do with the Psychic ability that I developed as I grew older, who knows.

Her mother Annie from Burton on Trent in Staffordshire apparently was not so nice. She met Mace on his travels and ran away with him. He worshiped her, a tiny woman she was very grand and refused to do housework, delegating her daughters the jobs she thought were beneath her.

Grandmother Major was glamorous. To me anyway, by the time I'd arrived my grandparents had retired. When she went out, even to the shops she always wore a mink coat and her diamond rings and lipstick, she was fun. She loved Music, going to the music hall and theatre, a big fan of Max Miller and Vera Lynn. She enjoyed a drink Brandy and Port being her tipple or a Guinness.

She would sometimes meet up with my other grandmother and friends in the Chalk Farm Tavern (in Primrose hill not Chalk farm) late afternoon for a drink in 'The Snug', a bar suitable for women on their own lodged between the saloon bar and the Public bar. It wouldn't have been done in those days for a lady to venture into the other bars without her husband.

She was always short of money. Despite the trappings she never had much cash. My grandfather who always carried at least £1000 in his back pocket to buy stock with for the shops was a bit mean with the housekeeping money. Generous in public and with friends, (but never flash at all, that wasn't his way) he gave her very little money to run the house on and bring up their children.

Consequently she was always robbing Peter to pay Paul and running up credit in the shops. Often as children we would be sent over to the off licence or grocers with a list and a letter saying please give Jeremy or Deborah such and such and put it on my bill. It never bothered me, but my mother hated it when she was a girl and vowed she'd never let a man keep her short of money or ever buy anything on credit. Ridiculous situation in this day and age but not uncommon then. She was too proud to ask for more money and probably too scared so this is how she lived, sadly.

It didn't stop her enjoying herself though. She'd have her friends around for tea in the afternoon. One of them Mavis was the local prostitute, I don't think my grandmother could have known this though as she would have been shocked, but my aunt Pat who was a closet lesbian and also great fun knew, and years later told me that Mavis had made a lot of money from a gentleman in the city, who used to hire her and other chorus girls to dress up as chickens with feathers strategically placed, while they walked around him in a circle, clucking while he pleasured himself. We thought it was hilarious.

My grandmother was a great cook and during the war she could produce great meals even during rationing. Obviously they were never short of vegetables or fruit. Years later when we had moved to Edgware, She used to bake an enormous lemon meringue pie to bring to Sunday lunch. My grandfather used to drive up the Edgware road with this huge meringue strapped to the roof rack. Too big to go in the boot it was a funny sight.

MY MAJOR UNCLE'S.

Character's all of them in their own way.

Ronnie was very handsome. My mother's eldest brother had matinee idol looks. He could have his pick of women and did. There were a lot of very happy married ladies in the St John's Wood area that thought very highly of him.

Tony was another good looker and a good business man.

Colin "The artful dodger" during the war he used to stand outside Chalk Farm tube station as a little boy wearing a top hat escorting people home in the blackout and smog for cash of course. (Another business man)

Edward (Teddy) another ladies man I'm afraid. Teddy and Tony were air stewards for 'The United Arab airlines' and looked very attractive in their uniforms. Women threw themselves at them especially Teddy who never said no.

None of them were angels and like most young boys got themselves into various scrapes but nothing too serious. They were a colourful lot and when they were altogether at my grandmothers around the table, it was a very "Italian" atmosphere. They were all quite loud and spoke with their hands and the main topic of conversation was food, how to cook it where to get it that sort of thing. They all loved to play cards too, only for pennies with a game called Solo being popular and five card brag. There are rumours of Italian blood on my great grandmother Majors side.

Pat.

My mother's younger sister was a larger than life character. As a young girl Ann Patricia got molested twice. Once over Primrose hill and the second time seriously by a man who lived around the corner in Chalcott Square. It's only recently that Paedophilia has become part of the national language. Back then there were just dirty old men. This paedophile who abused Pat badly, got sentenced to prison. When he was released he returned to his flat in Chalcott Square and carried on his life. This was never talked about in the family, it was considered too shameful. Poor Pat was never offered any counselling or anything. I'm surprised my grandfather didn't seek him out for a bit of revenge. My uncles were too young as otherwise they would have paid him a visit I'm sure.

These assaults had a profound effect on her and although it didn't show then, in later life she had to fight many demons including alcohol addiction.

She became a tough 'Tomboy' She would stage boxing matches with her brothers in the Airy (the basement of the house) She also used to fight boys for money on Chalk Farm Bridge approach. My uncles would take bets on her. She always won.

In her adult life she was a closet lesbian. I'm sure for years she didn't believe she was, she didn't find men particularly attractive but then considering what happened to her as a child it's not surprising.

She lived alone at the top of my grandmother's house in a flat. Before going to work at the home office as a civil servant, she'd have a few glug's and gargle in scotch. She used to tell me it opened her tubes, whatever that meant.

I lived with her for a while, my mother was taken into hospital for a hysterectomy and it went badly wrong it was touch and go. Poor mum suffered a lot in those days with what was only ever referred to as women's problems.

Hospitalised several times for different things, this time it was going to be for a long duration.

We had moved out to Edgware now it's about 1967/8 I was seven years old and had just got settled into a new school Stag Lane Junior. My father still worked in Camden Town and my sister Deborah went to Parliament Hill School in North London so they used to catch the tube in together but meant there was no one there to look after me.

So I went to stay with Auntie Pat, although you didn't dare call her auntie or indeed my uncle's uncle, if you did you'd get a clip around the ear. It was always first names. Unusual for the time.

I went back to Primrose hill school, where the headmaster and teachers were very kind to me as they knew how ill my mum was. My dad used to walk up to the school from work every lunchtime to meet me and take me over the road to the sweet shop and bring me a pack lunch. It was a confusing and worrying time for a little boy.

However, I had a lovely time with Pat. She spoilt me rotten. If you can picture Hattie Jacques in 'Carry on Matron' that was Pat. We would sit and listen to her Judy Garland, Shirley Bassey and Dorothy Squires records together. She would let me have a sip of her Whiskey and a puff on her cigarette. My mother would have gone ballistic if she knew. Our favourite snack was slices of garlic sausage from the deli wrapped around a hot chip.

Someone she met in the pub, her favourite was 'The Black Cap' in Camden Town a notorious gay pub (where the legendary Mrs Shufflewick the drag artist used to have a residency) had given her a canary. This canary had no feathers on it whatsoever and looked like it would die anytime. Anyway every morning before she went to work and me to school, she would put on the Lp of 'the Sound of Music', the beginning bit where the birds sing. This was to encourage Tabitha (the Canary) to get its voice back. It used to make a noise which was more like a dog barking. Part of Tabitha's recovery programme included a glug of scotch in her water tray, Pat figured if it could clear her tubes then it would work for Tabitha. Well you'd think she would have finished it off, but no in about two weeks Tabitha had grown back all her feathers and could sing like, well a canary!

When Tabs died Pat was distraught she laid her out in a large Cooks match box lined with cotton wool and dressed in full mourning black, took the poor thing down to the Regent canal where she poured lighter fuel over the box and gave Tabitha a Viking funeral. Crying her eyes out she watched Tabitha sail off into the sunset.

It was even worse when Judy Garland died. Pat wore black for ages but the first week she didn't go to work, she wouldn't let anyone into her flat and all you could hear was 'Judy Live at Carnegie Hall' over and over again. I was very young when I was first introduced to "Camp"

Deborah and i With grandad Major and mum

6 Chaimberlain Street where i was
born ground floor window.

Aged 11 with my cat Sacha

Deborah Aunty Pat and me 1963

Deborah, me with cousins
Joanne David and Syd.

Goodchild Grandparents

Lynn Rixon and Anne cotterill

Me about 18 months seaside

Me and mum with grandparents
Major in Edgware garden

Me sunday mirror reporter

Primrose hill school

Mum dad me and Nana
Major isle of wight

Suzanne, me and Deborah
Regents pk

3

A FATAL STABBING

Although this was an innocent time and street violence was not common, there was a terrible incident in 1964.

In Regents Park road we had a family run dairy with one of those old fashioned vending milk machines outside. It was owned and run by a Welsh family called Griffiths. Everybody went there for milk, cheese etc, the family were well liked and very friendly and kind. The Son Irwin I particularly remember. A jolly man, who had a crush on my mother I gather, used to serve behind the counter.

On Boxing Day December 26th a gang of 14 youths had been drinking in a pub in Kentish Town. Someone heard there was a party at a flat in Regents Park Road and these yobs decided to gate crash it. When they got to the address they were refused entry. So in retaliation they pulled out the crates of glass milk bottles which were stacked up at the dairy next door and proceeded to hurl the bottles at the window of the party flat breaking the windows and also of the shop next door.

Irwin the milkman ran out to see what was going on tried to stop the trouble, where the feral gang turned on him head butting him, kicked and knifed him in the groin. A young man in the flat below the party called Michael Joseph Munnelly (23) went out to help and chased the van and managed to get hold of the driver who screamed for help. The other yobs jumped out of the back of the van and proceed to kick Michael Munnelly a 'Sunday People' journalist to death. The poor man was awarded the Binney medal posthumously.

Although in this day and age it wouldn't even make the news in 1964 it was a big deal and shocked and disgusted everybody in the local community. As well as the poor dead man Irwin was very popular and I can remember seeing his beaten up bruised face as he continued to work behind the counter. I was only 4 years old. Irwin never recovered; he was never the same man. They sold up in 1970 and moved away from the area.

4

CELEBRITIES AND GENTRIFICATION

In the 1990's Primrose Hill became synonymous with the "Primrose Hill set "consisting of in 2019 the super rich Like Jamie Oliver wife Jules and Labour politicians like David Milliband. Jude Law, his wife Sadie Frost, Kate Moss, Liam Gallagher Dawn French etc.

It always had its fair share of famous people. In the 1960's besides Cilla there was Joan Bakewell, the playwright Alan Bennett, although technically Alan Bennett was Camden Town as he lived in Gloucester Crescent, a smart road but not Primrose hill. He lived opposite the Millers. Jonathan Miller was on TV with Alan and was also a playwright and theatre director. Lots of playwrights and authors lived in Gloucester terrace. Theatre people and musicians like George Melly and his family.

They were all very well educated people who had been to Oxbridge and attended private schools. They were all staunch Labour voters or communists and although having had the advantages of a private education, they did not believe in it, and sent their own children to the state schools, like Primrose Hill where I went, or chose selective comprehensive schools out of the borough. Pimlico Comprehensive was one of the favourites, if they didn't consider the local state schools to be good enough. So not quite as enthusiastic for all state schools for their own children. Like many Labour politicians of today.

According to William Miller (Jonathan's son) in his book 'Gloucester Terrace' their children were often bullied relentlessly at the state schools for being too posh. Their parents didn't realise it was happening and would have been shocked to think that they were considered posh or upper class, as they considered themselves 'of the people' as socialists. Today they would be called the metropolitan elite and leading the remain camp to stay in the EU.

They were a sort of modern day 'Bloomsbury group' that moved into NW1 and started buying up the houses cheaply and gentrifying them. Pushing up prices so that local people couldn't afford to stay there. Ironic for socialists really.

There were lots of actors and actresses in the area to.

The great comedienne Beryl Reid was a common sighting who always smiled and said good morning. Another Comic actress Peggy Mount who was a lesbian and who had a girlfriend who worked in the dry cleaners in Regents Park Road. A tiny quiet little woman who wouldn't say boo to a goose. Peggy the complete opposite was known for her large stature and big booming voice. She was a huge star in the 1960's in TV shows such as Hugh and I with Hugh Lloyd. As well as actors many media types started moving in.

In the 1960's property in Primrose hill was still relatively cheap by some central London standards. Still showing a few scar's from the war you could bag a large house for about 5-10 thousand pounds. A lot of money then but not for actors and BBC types or as we call them these days "Luvvies."

A well known cartoonist called Mark Boxer nicknamed these people "The Stringalongs" based on Alan Bennett's 1960's TV series "on the margin". Mainly professionals or media people they would buy an old house and knock through the rooms turning the basements into one large kitchen where they would sit around their obligatory pine scrubbed tables and put the world to rights. The Miliband brothers remember sitting underneath their parent's kitchen table listening to all the famous communists of the day discussing poverty and deprivation. A bit ironic seeing they were living in Primrose Hill.

My mother recalls this patronising arty woman holding forth in Alderson's the Chemists (where we all went to tell Mr Alderson of our ailments) that they, the new residents were moving in to try and "give something to the community, to develop the area and improve it" My mother told her "there is nothing wrong with the area, it has always been a nice area with a friendly local community, we don't need your idea of improvements thank you."

Which it was, there were a few houses that were a bit tatty and some evidence of war damage but overall it was a nice friendly respectable area. Most people rented rooms or apartments and the landlord's then were not enthusiastic about spending money on improvements, however the rents ere quite low.

Ironically what these do-gooders and socialists did was break up the local community completely. Many people saw the ridiculous bucks these professionals were willing to pay them and thought they were laughing all the way to the bank. My own family included. So sadly by the 1980's the Primrose Hill I grew up in didn't exist anymore.

Now unfortunately a lot of the property is owned by multi billionaires, foreign bankers from Russia, China etc and left empty just like Notting hill and other areas of London.

A house you could buy for 10k in 1966 would now cost you 4.5 million pounds and upwards.

5

THE LADY IN THE VAN

Although not strictly Primrose Hill. Miss Shepherd is worth mentioning. Dame Maggie Smith made her famous in the play and then the film of Alan Bennett's 'The Lady in the van.' This local eccentric tramp was allowed by Alan Bennett to put the old van (painted with yellow emulsion) that she lived in, temporarily in Alan Bennett's front garden in Gloucester terrace. What was supposed to be a 3 month stayover lasted for 15 years. As children we remember seeing her sitting outside the bank in Parkway selling her pencils. A large woman, my sister Deborah found her quite frightening and had nightmares about her. Our mother on nice evenings would walk us down Parkway in Camden town to Albany street where Curry and Paxton's the optical firm was to meet my father after work. Miss Shepherd would be sitting there writing her predictions on the pavement.

It turned out that after she accidentally hit somebody in a car she went into hiding not reporting the crime. She had been an ambulance driver during the blackout in the war. Before that she had been an esteemed concert pianist. She was also a devout Roman Catholic and decided she wanted to become a Nun. It was during this period that one of the "Superior" Nuns told her that playing the piano was forbidden as it would offend God. So she never played again and shunned music. What a waste of talent. Nuns can be so cruel sometimes. There was a convent at the top of Parkway and

Miss Shepherd never went far away from them, even though they said she wasn't suitable to be "one of them" So she spent her life living in a van and praying to God. Eventually she died in it and Alan Bennett had to dispose of what was left. This was how he was able to trace her family and find out about her.

6

PROSTITUTION AND EXTORTION

In the 1960's There was a certain type of landlord the most famous being Peter Rachman who used to buy up houses and force people out by putting undesirables into the houses /flats as neighbours. Usually prostitutes or rough types. Once the people could stand it no longer they would often move out leaving the flats empty so the owners/ landlords would sell them the houses cheaply to get out and move on.

This man, it may have been Rachman, tried this on in Primrose hill in Chamberlain Street, our street. A house next door but one to us was used. He put prostitutes in a flat, while the other flats were occupied by families. Our good friends Gladys and Bob lived in one of them. The police used our sitting room at number 6 to watch the goings on.

Eventually one of his men tried to put the muscle on my family. Now my family didn't own the house then. Like a lot of people my grandfather had a lifetime rental agreement on the house at a peppercorn rent. People like my grandparents then used to rent out parts of the house to lodgers thus living rent free and able to cover their bills. Quite clever really but they were the generation that didn't believe in buying property.

This "Rachman type chap," approached the landlords of the house to buy it for a good price, meanwhile threatening the tenants that unless they got out they would flood the street with prostitutes and undesirables. However they had underestimated my mother. One of them turned up on the door step and threatened her. Now my mother is always a lady and never swears, but she was able to look him straight in the eye and tell him very firmly that men like him would never frighten her and that she'd never give in to intimidation or threats, just who did he think he was? He said yes I can see that and walked away.

So my mother convinced my father and grandparents that the only way to beat them in the long run was to buy the house from the landlords. So with their agreement my mother agreed a price with the landlords (about £6.000) and managed to get a joint mortgage based on my father and grandfathers earnings, quite a thing in the 1960's.

People wouldn't deal with a woman without their husband's permission. Unbelievable but true. A woman couldn't get a hire purchase agreement without her husband signing his permission. So my mother did well. Also by letting the police use our sitting room for surveillance they were soon able to make arrests and put an end to to the bully boy's shenanigans. An early feminist victory I suppose.

7

Off to Suburbia

After a few years our house had risen considerably in value. My grandparents were retired and wanted to move out to Enfield to live with their younger son Leslie and his wife Eileen. Leslie and Eileen had bought a house with a large plot and massive garden. My grandfather a very keen Gardner wanted to spend his old age growing vegetables and why not. In Primrose Hill we only had back yards basically not very big. So in 1967 that's what happened we sold up. The grandparents bought a mobile home and had it put on the land in Enfield where they spent the rest of their days. We, after lots of searching ended up in Edgware. Top of north London. Staying in Primrose Hill was now out of the question. The price of property was shooting through the roof with all the BBC and media types moving in. My parents split the profit with my grandparents and used that as a deposit for a new house. So we had to, like a lot of other people reluctantly move further out. The one thing that was paramount was that we stayed on the northern line tube so my sister Deborah could carry on going to parliament hill school which was a grammar school then. She was 13 and doing very well, I on the other hand was only 7 so I was sent to the local primary school Stag Lane Junior. I adapted quickly, making new friends straight away. Just up the road were two girls Lynn Rixon and Anne Cotterill. These two became my best buddies and stayed friends for many years. We've lost contact with Anne but Lynn and I are still in touch 50+ years later.

So my happy childhood continued. I liked my new school had good friends and we were always out playing marbles or riding our bikes and treat of the week, Saturday morning pictures. For six-pence (3p) parents could send their kids off to the local Odeon cinema were we would watch all these lovely old films. They used to have competitions and talent contests that sort of thing. We were always noisy and the usherettes used to be like prison guards shining the torch in your face and telling you to shut up, it was hilarious. Afterwards we always went to the Wimpy bar in Burnt oak for a plate of chips or if one of us were well off a burger. I never liked Wimpy burgers and always had a Bender and chips. (I know!) this was a frankfurter with incisions made in it so that it would curl into a circle in hot water, they'd put that on the bun with some pan yan pickle and a slice of tomato in the middle, it was delicious.

Cinema then was our main outside entertainment. The whole family would go to see the latest James Bond film together or if it was a special treat 'The sound of Music' or similar at Leicester Square Odeon. Sometimes we would go and see a Variety show at the London Palladium. We would climb up into the God's and see the headline acts of the day like Des O'Connor, Jimmy Tarbuck and Val Doonican plus a host of other acts. I loved that and I miss "Variety" it's a shame it doesn't exist now.

I was doing very well at Stag Lane Junior, my grades were good. I was particularly good at English, music of course and I loved history. I was never any good at maths, but I'm eternally grateful for those teachers (Mrs Fox we were terrified of her) drumming into us our times tables. We had to sit there every day chanting two twos are four three twos are six etc, over and over until we could do it in our sleep, and if nothing else sank in much that and division have helped me out on so many occasions as an adult.

I was never really naughty then, cheeky probably. I enjoyed school; history particularly fascinated me, especially the Tudor period. I'd started off on my own back, to compile a scrap book of relative articles and paste them into my book, anything I could find pertaining to the Tudors. It was a hobby and nothing to do with school work. One day I was naughty and was sent to sit outside the headmistress's office. Miss Wood hadn't been at the school long and nobody liked her. Anyway, I was sat there writing notes in my scrap book and she came out and picked it up and ridiculed it, said it was rubbish that sort of thing. She was really nasty, I've never forgotten it. With that I threw the scrap book in the waste bin and my attitude changed overnight.

From being an ideal pupil I became a mini James Dean. From now on I'd always be in trouble of some sort. Always getting caught smoking, I used to bury them in the garden in an old Golden Virginia tobacco tin of my fathers. This worked well until he decided to dig over the garden and I got caught and received a good hiding. I'm about 8 or 9 years old now. That head teacher had turned me into a rebel. I only got the cane once (later on) and that was for something I didn't do which made me even more angry and rebellious. Except for that blip it was a very happy time.

On Saturdays we used to have a green grocer called 'Dirty Dick' who came around the streets with a horse and cart. He'd have all the veg and fruit (usually past its sell by date) piled on the back of the cart. He used to let us kids hop on the front and ride around the block with him, which of course we all loved. He got the name "Dirty Dick" because when you were riding upfront with him he always used to try to cop a feel of one of us, boys included. Nowadays there would be riots but we just used to laugh it off.

At the end of the chase a girl called Yvonne lived, we all became friendly with her. She had striking looks and was tall and a bit older than us. She seemed sophisticated as she always had a packet of cigarettes on her which she would share out. One day she invited me into her house. Her mother came down the stairs with barely a stitch on and said in a sultry voice, "Jeremy come here I want you" I was terrified and scarpered out of the front door, I could hear the two of them in fits of laughter as I ran away. Turns out she was the local Prostitute. She used to entertain clients at home while

Yvonne was there, which was very wrong as Yvonne couldn't have been more than 12 herself.

The most colourful neighbour we had was an Irish Lady Called Mrs Milligan. She was glamour personified, she used to wear one of those great big sun hats, and her makeup would be put on very heavily with bright red lipstick and big kohl surround eyes. She was as blind as a bat so it was a bit hit and miss. She had long curled dyed blonde hair like Veronica Lake the actress. Looking back she was gorgeous but then as kids and in that area she stood out like a sore thumb. She'd worn high heels for so long that she couldn't put her feet down flat on the floor, this fascinated me. She'd be in the front garden with her sun hat on, slip on high heels and a flower basket over her arm singing to herself as she clipped roses for the house. So unusual a sight was she that as kids, I'm ashamed to admit we used to taunt her and call her names and take the mickey out of her. She never retaliated but one day she came over to see my mother for a chat, I suppose about my behaviour. My mum and she hit it off straight away; she was very well spoken with a soft Irish Lilt and terribly sophisticated. Ann and her lovely gentle husband called Pop had fallen on hard times and had ended up in Edgware by default a bit like us. Pop drove a Mr Whippy ice cream van to make ends meet, which his daughters Olivia and Ingrid thought was hilarious. They were grown up and quite the girls about town, having editors of daily newspapers and Persian princes as boyfriends, however they still lived at home, they were both gorgeous and great fun.

Ann Milligan invited my family over for drinks. Their house was very grand for a semi detached and you could see the expensive articles remaining from a previous life on show. Ann never did accept her reduced circumstances and lived as she had always lived, much to the consternation of Pop. Ann became a great friend to all of us. She always spoke to me as if I was an adult and never a child which I greatly appreciated. I shall never forget her and was very fond of her. Eventually they escaped to Golders Green and had a summer home on the coast in Goring in West Sussex.

8

A FIRST YEAR AGAIN

I failed the 11 plus unfortunately, I was considered "borderline" grammar school but didn't quite make it. Due to maths probably. So I was going to be sent to this really rough school in Edgware. It had a terrible name. I did not want to go there. My mother fought tooth and nail to get me a place somewhere else, it wasn't easy and luckily I got accepted into Chandos All Boys School in Stanmore Middlesex which had a reputation for high standards in musical education. With my ability to play several instruments plus my voice still soprano at the time I was a natural fit for the school. The only problem was it meant a lot of travelling.

I used to have to walk about a mile to Burnt Oak Coop and catch a 140 bus from there to the nearest stop to the school about 30 minutes, then there was another long walk to the school through a park. The school is now known as Park High and is a mixed comprehensive. I was often late due to the buses and they used to put a prefect at the entrance to the school gate to take your name. Then you'd have to do 15 minutes detention after school. I was a regular. Until I learnt that you could jump over a gate in the park into the side of the school and sneak in there, they got wise to this and used to have another prefect stationed there. You had to be quick.

I was pleased to find another boy who lived near me there called Keith Jacobs so we used to travel in together. There was this little shop on the way to school run by a Pakistani man. He used to sell us children loose cigarettes for a penny each. Keith used to spend his dinner money on the fags so we could have a smoke on the way to school and I used to split my pack lunch with him. My mother always made loads so it was fine. I always had the best sandwiches, lots of salad, fruit, chocolate, crisps etc. Other kids with a bit of fish paste on 'Mothers Pride' thin bread used to stare in amazement on my big chunky sandwiches packed with ham salad and sandwich spread mayo.

I soon settled into school life. It was very different. Now we were the small fry and there were the big boys, real bullies some of them. They had an initiation ceremony at Chandos known as giving you "The Rack" The big boys would get hold of the first years, 11 year olds and get them up against these metal bars that were at the end of the playground and hitch a little kid up onto it and stretch his arms over the top bar while the other boys grabbed the poor boys legs and pulled them back under the bottom bar and stretch him until he screamed in agony. I was really lucky as I never got this. I was threatened often but I used to hide.

Then as time went on I got really friendly with some of the girls. Although Chandos was an all boy's school, it had a girl's school in the same building. We were separated by doors inside and a line down the middle of the playground and that was it.

Skinhead culture was at its peak. In 1971-2 there were lots of skinhead boys at Chandos, the older ones used to get away with wearing their "cool" Sta pressed and two tone tonic trousers. They wore red socks and the shoes were either loafers with tassels or what were known as basket weave shoes. Shirts had to be Ben Sherman or Brutus with a carefully ironed pleat down the back. Braces usually red to hold the trousers up high so you could see the red socks and the shiny shoes. Coats were always Crombies with a little red hanky showing and a diamante tie pin stuck in the pocket of the coat. Often this was topped off with a trilby hat. Of course the hair was shaved down to a number one all over. Everyone also used to stink of the mens after shave Brut, even the girls. The girls would have these tiny bottles of it in their handbags and the boys in their Crombie coat pockets. They were 10 shillings (50p) from boots. A lot of money then.

I loved the look although my mother would not let me have my head shaved, she'd say the only children that do that have nits!

However, eventually I was allowed to have a pair of two tone tonic trousers from Wembley market. An old Crombie coat that had belonged to my uncle and given to him by a child actor of the 1940's called Jeremy Spencer, that's how old it was, but it was a beautiful coat. My dad bought me a pair of basket weave shoes. We used to put metal blakey's in the heel so they tapped when you walked along so people could see you were wearing cool shoes. However I was sworn to secrecy over the cost. My dad went alone with me to buy them and he made me swear on the bus home to never tell my mother what they cost (they were expensive) I never did.

Even trying to blend in I was sometimes called a poof etc. I suppose I was a bit different, I was quite loud and cocky and probably a bit flamboyant. I didn't realise any of this at the time. I was always in love with some girl. To avoid getting the rack and beaten up, I made friends with the coolest girl in school called Kim Prowen, she was a card. She would fight the boys, wear a trilby hat and was well known amongst the skinhead girls. She was tough and everyone was frightened of her, even the teachers. I wasn't though and we hit it off and became best friends. When we were older we even had a bit of a romance. Innocent but we did love each other. So Kim was my protection. Anyone that threatened me would have Kim to deal with; she would beat them up if they so much as looked at me the wrong way.

We and all the other cool kids used to meet at a bench up on the line that divided the schools in the playground. Here we'd sit surreptitiously smoking, we all smoked then, always getting told off or getting detention for smoking.

Some boys got whipped with the cane 6 lashes at times. One teacher used to love assembling about 6 metal rulers together and would get the boy to put his hand out while he thrashed it holding these rulers from as high away as he could to inflict the maximum amount of pain, some of those teachers were absolute bastards really wicked!

However, we carried on regardless, laughing, planning our weekend parties. Listening to music on our transistor radios and portable cassette tape players, learning dance steps etc. I couldn't wait for the bell to go so I could get back up on the line with Kim and my other great friend Carol Bond. They were both older than me by a couple of years. Thankfully I never got into a fight and I never got beaten up, result.

Music was everything to us. Tamla Motown was huge and we loved Marvin Gaye, Jimmy Ruffin, Stevie Wonder and Diana Ross but our other big love was Reggae. We loved Desmond Decker Prince Buster, songs like 'Long Shot kick the bucket,' 'Love of the common people,' 'Skinhead moon stomp' all those old hits. When the pop group Slade came along we felt they represented us. We were not into glam Rock at all, Queen, David Bowie were not our type. Just a bunch of poufs we thought. But Slade were for the skinheads. I never was one but I was a wannabe for sure. We worshipped Slade. We'd go to someone's house at lunchtime and listen to the charts and pray they would go straight to number one with their new hit. They always did. They were hugely successful. I managed to see them at Earls court, right at the back but it didn't matter I was with my heroes. I was completely deaf for about 3 days afterwards. In fact I think it damaged my hearing for life they were so loud. (I've got hearing aids now for god's sake!)

It wasn't all mucking about I was doing well at Chandos. Even in English which is a surprise. I was always good at it but our poor young English teacher was often in tears at the boys antics, or she'd catch them deliberately masturbating in the front row, sometimes each other. (Well it was an all boy's school) Adolescent boys need strict older teachers, young girls straight out of teacher training college is asking for trouble. She was lovely though Miss Morgan and I did learn from her while she lasted.

Music was the big thing. I was in the choir and we used to tour around Harrow and some big arenas in London to join up with other school choirs to perform concerts. These were big affairs and we'd perform Handel's Messiah and other big classical pieces. We even made a record I loved it. The feeling you get singing with hundreds of others is amazing. I had a good voice. I was also in the brass band learning the trumpet. I was in the woodwind group, learning various recorders and the saxophone. Chandos really was great for music. The main music teacher a Mr Leslie Tucker was very strict, round as a barrel and you didn't mess with him at all.

My mother approached him to give me private piano lessons at home. I was mortified. I used to have to wait for him after school every Tuesday and get into his Rover car and drive out of the school gates passing all the other boys on their way home. I used to cringe with embarrassment as they all pointed and took the mickey. I can't put into words really what a horrible ordeal that was at the time, especially as I hung out with a cool gang.

However he was a really nice man and he did teach me and well at home. He started me off at grade 3 level bypassing 1 and 2 which I passed easily. Then we worked for about a year and I passed grade 4. I was just about to take grade 5 when we moved, but I'll come to that later. I always have played by ear without music. I can read music obviously; otherwise I wouldn't have passed those grades which are quite tough. But I used to learn the fixed pieces I had to play by heart and then play them and turn the page at the right moment so the examiners thought I was reading it properly. I never needed to, once a piece was in my head after learning it from reading, it stayed in there. Often in music group at school Mr Tucker would say "come on Goodchild finish the lesson and play us a medley of old songs" I used to get up and play all the old pub songs I'd learned as a child. 'My old man', 'Maybe it's because I'm a Londoner' all those sort of things and we'd have a sing-along. Most of the kids knew those songs too as they'd all grown up in London. It was fun.

Around this time or just before my mother was working at the London American School in Regents Park running the tuck shop for these super wealthy American kids. The woman who ran the school called me in one day and asked me to sing to her. My mother had been bragging about my voice and musical ability I suppose. She was very highly connected and she got someone else to listen to me. On the back of this I was offered a scholarship as a boy soprano, at St Pauls School and Westminster. I'll never know what that could have led to as my father refused to let me go because they were both weekly boarding schools and he refused to let me stay away from home.

I understand that but I always wonder what might have been, I could have been Prime minister? The only thing I gained from regular visits to the American school was a lifelong love of clam chowder soup.

At that time it was mainly white kids at Chandos. We had black boys and all skinheads too, and they ruled the roost. Nobody would mess with them. I was ok because they all loved Kim. One of them known as 'Chopper' who looked fierce, all muscle and attitude was lovely to me took me under his wing a bit which was also good for my street cred.

Indians were starting to arrive and Pakistanis. They stood out more because they didn't mix much especially with each other. The Sikhs would stand together in one part of the playground. The Hindus another and the Pakistanis and Muslims on the opposite side of the playground. They never mixed. The Jewish kids of which there were quite a lot, being in the Stanmore and Edgware area, got excused attending school assembly but other than that blended in with the rest of us. Even then people wanted to stay within their own tribes.

Lunchtimes were party times, if we were not meeting at "the line" we'd head over to one of the boys houses that lived locally. I'd drag my mum's shopping trolley onto the 140 bus with me full of 45 rpm records. My best male friend was a Greek Cypriot boy called Pantilakis Solomou. Pandy as he was known was a lovely boy and the youngest child of older parents. His older sister lived up the road and her daughter Lita, another great friend who was older than Pandy, was one of the coolest girls at schools and loved all of us. We'd often go to Pandy's house at lunchtime. His dad worked in a restaurant in the west end somewhere and everyday he'd bring home pounds of ham off the bone and a litre bottle of Emva Cream sherry. His mother also worked so we had the house to ourselves. We'd all pool our packed lunches and turn them into buffets, crack open the sherry and demolish all the ham. The old radio gram would be ramped up and we would dance away to all the latest hits and get pissed on the sherry. If it was someone else's house we'd raid the parent's drinks cabinets and make cocktails. We never ever took drugs. However a couple of times we over did it and went back to school drunk. We had this technical drawing teacher called Mr Chandler who would look at me and say 'Goodchild I think you'd better go and sit at the back and sleep it off,' Chalky as we called him never reported it and we got away with it all for ages.

Most weekends I was in Primrose hill visiting my grandparents and Auntie Pat. I loved going back, I'd see my friends occasionally Jane and Karen Prior, twins who lived in Regents park road and their older sister Lesley. Lesley was cool because she had a mohair suit and wore loafers. She taught me how to smoke (I kid her about this) and how to get money out of the old A and B phone box on the corner of Regents Park Road and St Georges terrace where I had gone for piano lessons aged 4. The old public phones worked like this, you put your money in and pushed button A when the person answered, Then when you'd finished the call you'd push button B to get any change left. Some people didn't bother so you could get a few pennies by pushing button B. Also if you gave the phone a good thump in the middle the money would come out. Handy if you were running short of fags or sweets. One day we did this and Lesley bought a packet of No 6 cigarettes, a cheap but popular brand at the time and took us rowing over Regents Park boating lake, where we moored up and had a smoke.

Most times I'd be at Berkley Road with my family. As I got older after saying hello to my grandparents I'd sneak upstairs to Pats flat who was much more fun. She'd usually be sitting with her friend who lived in the flat underneath Madeleine, They were usually ploughing they're way through a bottle of scotch.

I loved to listen to all the gossip and the stories and I'd get the occasional drink and fag as well, which made me feel grown up. I was always older than my years anyway and always appreciated being treated like an adult. However Pat got to attached to Madeleine and vice versa and Madeleine's husband a big Irish builder also called Pat got very upset and they moved away. Our Pat was going to be named in the eventual divorce, but it came to nothing thank god.

However sadly in 1971 this all came to an end. My lovely grandmother Nanny Major had a massive brain haemorrhage. She was in hospital for 6 months. My mother went to visit her every day. After catching the tube and changing several times to get to South London (where she was now working for my uncles as a secretary in their successful garage business) she would make her way back up to the Hampstead General or whatever hospital my grandmother was in.

She would see to her mother and help her the best way she could, and then get the tube home to us walking miles from the tube station to get us an evening meal. I don't know how she did it. She was and is an amazing woman.

My grandmother did make some progress and learned how to speak again. They had to shave off her lovely auburn hair and put her in a wig. Her speech was slurred but she was a toughie and she came to stay for a while when they let her out of hospital. However this recovery didn't last long and she died aged only 67.

It was my first death and it had a profound effect on me. The grief in our house was heavy. My grandmother was the real matriarch of us all and her children couldn't cope. Pat couldn't even make it to the funeral. Inevitably all the responsibility fell on my mother's shoulders. Luckily our dear aunt Nel was staying with us at the time. She had lost her big sister but she was able to help us a lot with our grief.

My grandmother who was quite a large woman had got addicted to slimming pills, speed in other words. It was the 60's 70's and black bombers were easily available. She'd get prescription pills, and then my uncles used to get her more as she wanted nobody then realised the dangers of them. I expect she would take them to give her energy. She had quite a hard life sometimes. Nobody knew they were addictive. This and her penchant for a drop of brandy caused her blood pressure to soar and this is what caused the brain haemorrhage we think now. Addiction runs in families but in those days nobody knew anything about much.

My grandfather couldn't cope; he developed diabetes and then got dementia. It was awful we had to put him in a home which broke my mother's heart, but there really wasn't a choice. He had really loved my grandmother and he never got over it, he followed her two years later. At his funeral tea at our house afterwards, this big Rolls Royce pulled up outside of the house and this huge man who looked like my grandfather came up the drive to the house. It turned out this was my step or half uncle; my grandfather had been married before and had four other sons. My mother only found out when she was grown up and we were never told.

It turns out that my grandparents didn't get married until the 1950's so all of their children were illegitimate or bastards as they called them then. The stigma and shame years ago was terrible and it was all hushed up. I never met the others but Uncle John came into our lives for a brief period. He was a successful publican and owned 'The Wilton Arms' pub in Dawes Road Fulham. he was known to one and all as "The Major."

If we hadn't gone "home" I'd inevitably be at someone's house for a party. Some of my friends had houses with conservatories which were ideal for teenage parties. Most of the parents allowed us to have cider. My parents would not have done. They were very strict about anything like that and had no idea what I was really getting up to. We all used to take a big bottle of cider with us and dance away smoking and getting plastered on cheap cider. Usually Woodpecker. We are now about 12-13.

9

'TOP OF THE POPS'

One of our gang Bobby Goodman's mum worked at the BBC. His sister Gigi had a crush on me, but I was head over heels in love with a beautiful looking girl called Sonia and wasn't really interested. Sonia was Greek and her parents were very strict, so it didn't go far. When Gigi asked me to go to 'Top of the Pops' with her my ears pricked up. Gigi's mum got us tickets and a few of us got the tube up to Shepherds Bush to the BBC and the 'Top of the pops 'studios.

'Top of the Pops' was a huge program then, millions of viewers. All the top stars would appear on it. Filmed on a Wednesday night it went out on air on Thursday night. We were supposed to be 16 but nobody asked that I remember and we were all herded in like cattle from outside into the studio. I can't describe what it was like, we were so excited. I thought I'd died and gone to heaven.

Tony Blackburn was the DJ presenter. We were all pushed around and told to dance to everything, even the Simon Park Orchestra who were number one with the theme from some TV show called Van der Valk, which was a bit awkward. Some of the acts we saw were Mud, The Sweet, Status Quo (who took the mickey out of my dancing in my flared dungarees.) Showoddywoddy Peters n Lee all sorts. It was Wonderful. It was even better on Friday morning and everyone at school had seen us on the telly. We felt like stars.

I went to 'Top of the Pops' on two or three more occasions, Dave lee Travis was the host on one and a really nice bloke, as was Tony

Blackman. The producers used to shout at us and treat us like dirt and you had to look out for the roving cameras or you'd go flying. Onetime we went and it was with Jimmy Saville presenting. At the time he was a massive star at the BBC. A friend of Royalty and a national treasure. On Top of the pops everyone tries to get near the DJ so that you would get your face on the telly.

However, he came up to us and said come and stand next to me I'll make you all stars. The two girls I was with giggled and we stood next to and behind him. He said to me "are you shagging both of them"? Now remember we are barely 13 and quite naive, we were in the 1970's. Next thing I know as they are setting up the next shot, his hand came from behind him and he grabbed my crotch. I was horrified but didn't know what to do. He said "you're a pretty one you are" Then he turned his attention to the girls and started touching their small adolescent breasts and saying let me rub them and make them grow that sort of thing. We didn't know what to do and just giggled nervously. All this was in front of the camera man who was getting ready to film the next introduction to the next group. We didn't tell our parents or anyone in authority we were to embarrassed. Back then we didn't know what a paedophile was. We only knew about dirty old men. I'm glad we got away from him.

Many years later when it came to light what a disgusting old pervert he was and what he got up to at the BBC and with the patients at Broadmoor hospital I was able to help the police with their enquires via Operation Yewtree. I did it because at the beginning no boys had come forward and it was assumed it was just little girls he molested. We soon started learning the truth. Lots of people knew what he was like and didn't say a thing and they let him get away with it for years. A very shameful part of our entertainment history.

10

A VILLAGE LIFE FOR ME

In 1974 my Parents had been looking for a business for two years. My mother wanted a pub and my father a shop. We looked at dozens and dozens of both. We looked at shops in Suffolk where we had family and we looked at pubs in Sussex. We ended up going for a pub in Sussex.

This was brought about because the great friends of ours from Primrose Hill the Priors (The twins, Lesley, Dolly and Wally etc) had decided to move out of London. They opened a map and with eyes closed got a pin and waived it over the map and stuck the pin in Brighton. They ended up buying a grocers shop in Montiefiore Road in Hove. We started going down for weekends which were always great fun with lots of parties and hilarity. Dolly used to love a house full and there were beds everywhere. Some weekends there were so many of us she used to do breakfast in two shifts! So we got to know Sussex quite well and that's where my mum and dad thought we should move to.

Always professional my parents paid to go on an expensive two week course for publicans at a training school in Donhead Dorset. There they learned how to run a pub properly. From catering to cellar management. It was an intensive course but stood them in great stead later. Also to gain experience they volunteered to work for free at local pubs at weekends. (landlords loved them)

One particular pub they worked in was a big pub in the Edgware Road in London. They worked the bar on their own for about 500 Irish people. I washed over 2,000 mainly Guinness glasses. I worked for hours I was only 12 and the tight manager gave me 10 shillings! 50p. It wasn't much then either. On a short break I was watching from the sidelines all the Irish dancing, it was great but from nowhere this great big Irishman lunged at me drunk, shoving his hands between my legs and groped me. I ran off and of course never told anyone.)

While they were away training I was farmed off to my great aunt Nel in Saxmundham in Suffolk which suited me. I had always got on with my aunt Nel, she was like a great friend to me, I adored her. She had lost two children tragically years before, which had caused her to have a breakdown. When she recovered she had two sons Roderick and Andrew. So I'd stay with them and her Husband Doug for holidays. Nellie and I would go out somewhere different every day. Catching the bus to Aldeburgh, Southwold, Lowestoft, Felixstowe, all the East Anglia seaside resorts. I loved it. Or we would cross the road to great aunt Berthas house and play cards. I used to sob when I left her and their gorgeous dog called Brett. I had a Black cat called Sacha but we were not allowed a dog. Brett was a real boy's dog and would follow you everywhere.

Eventually after many interviews and pub viewings my parents were offered The Talbot Inn in Cuckfield West Sussex near Haywards Heath, This was decided on because it was in a smart area had an upmarket clientele and was near Haywards Heath station so my sister could commute to work in the West End. I would have to change schools at 14.

A few days before we left I persuaded my girlfriend of the time to let me go "all the way "and I lost my virginity and took hers a few days before my 14th birthday aged 13. Like all boys I was desperate to do it and was as randy as hell all the time as you are at 13. It was not a very enjoyable experience and over pretty quickly.

At the time I was having a flirtatious crush with my dear friend Kim Prowen and also carrying on a long distance romance with my old friend Jane who I was extremely fond of. A bit complicated for a 13 year old! This intensified when a few weeks later my girlfriend in London phoned me to say she was pregnant. I was mortified. She wasn't she was just trying to keep me interested. I'm ashamed to say I went off her very quickly after we had done the deed. The other girls in my crowd offered to go around and sort her out which was dreadful in hindsight; I didn't let them I hasten to add.

Before I left my mum and dad paid for me to hire a hall and have a big farewell party. My sister (6 years older than me) and her Fiancé Brian were there to supervise. It was the usual teenage bash and my sister remembers lots of girls crying because I was leaving.

On the day we actually left 6 Greencourt Avenue in Edgware my dear friend Kim Prowen her pal Debbie and Anne and Lynn my girlfriend and a few others stood at the top of our drive to wave us off. As we pulled out of the drive in my dad's old Morris Minor, Jimmy Ruffin came on the radio singing 'Farewell is a lonely sound.' This was wonderful but a bit odd as this record was "The" record of my group of friends, including the twins down in Brighton. It was our anthem. We loved it and played it and danced to it for years. We still do. So it was peculiar that it came on the radio at that precise moment. It was very poignant and emotional. My friends were all crying as they waved me goodbye and I cried all the way to Sussex. I really did not want to go.

My mother could not understand why I was so upset. She had always hated Edgware. Coming from Primrose Hill and working in the west end, she had never been able to adapt to suburbia and loathed it. She refers to it now as "The boring years" Cuckfield offered an exciting change, running a pub a new challenge, more money, a completely different way of life. It was certainly that alright.

11

THE CUCKFIELD YEARS

We arrived to take over the tenancy of The Talbot Inn High street Cuckfield in West Sussex on July 5th 1974. I remember because it was the day before my 14th birthday and all my family forgot it. Our lives would change forever.

The Talbot was a lovely pub. One fairly large room with an off licence attached to it in the middle. Next to this was another door with a big wide staircase leading up to a large function hall that was known as the court room. This was because in the 1600's it was in fact the local court house. They used to try people in the court room and if necessary hang them in the street outside.

The Talbot had large living accommodation above. I had a really big bedroom all to myself. My sister bagged the top floor with another really good size bedroom and next to the bathroom. The 4th bedroom we converted into an upstairs kitchen for us to use separately from the catering kitchen downstairs. My parents had a large double next to mine.

Downstairs behind the bar was a good size catering kitchen with another scullery type room off of it. This led into a street level beer cellar and onto more outbuildings and a back yard. It was exciting exploring all this as a 14 year old. The outbuildings led into the old stables which also had rooms above full of trunks and costumes. Behind that was a locked door. It took me ages to find the key but when I did I got a surprise when I opened it.

Inside was a room with maps on the wall. With pins in and diagrams. There were posters depicting scenes from WW2. It looked as if it had been locked up after the war and not been touched. Eventually the mystery was solved. It had been a secret look out station in the war to watch out for German planes coming over to bomb us. There was a tunnel underneath that led directly to an underground bunker in the grave yard in the church which looked out over the Sussex downs. So these chaps would have been able to see the Germans coming over the sea and alerted the headquarters at Horsham first, who in turn notified London from this secret room. One night a group of men came in to the bar dressed in RAF uniforms a bit like 'Dads Army' All getting on a bit in years and asked for "the key" They explained they were a group called the Royal observer corps. A group of ex servicemen who had used the room for surveillance and still had regular meetings out in the stables from time to time. Founded on the 29/10/1925 they stayed in service until 31/03/1995. They remained throughout the cold war, using underground bunkers to measure the force of nuclear blasts should they happen. I gather they were reserved like the Territorial Army. The one in Cuckfield is still open to the public.

They were nice men very polite and smart. They used to get their pints of beer and go off to the secret room for a couple of hours. We never did find out what they discussed.

Another night I went down into the bar and it was full of lots of men and a few women dressed up as Roundheads and Cavaliers. It turned out our court room was the meeting place of the Local Sealed knot society. A group that meets to plan and re enact old battles. Some of the Cavaliers looked wonderful in their big red jackets and wide brimmed hats, adorned with big ostrich feathers. The roundheads not so much. Being Cromwellians they were dressed in sombre black. For a boy from the smoke like me it was a real eye opener. It was also good for business every Friday night.

The Talbot had lost its way a bit before we took over and the turnover wasn't great. Although, there were some good regular customers. Mainly top shelf, which is how we referred to spirit drinkers. Although legally I wasn't supposed to be behind the bar I'd always get roped in to wash glasses. In those days we did them all by hand. No glass washers. I was soon serving, making pink gins, gin and It (gin and dark vermouth) bloody Mary's, Babycham's and pet hate snowballs (Advocat and lemonade with a cherry). Old fashioned drinks but popular at the time. We didn't have ice machines and people then very rarely had ice in their drinks at all. Occasionally someone would ask for one piece of ice in a gin and tonic but very rarely, seems funny now when all our drinks come up to the brim with ice. Too much usually.

From day one mum started doing lunches. Everything homemade. All the pastry everything except for the bread.

It didn't take long for the word to get around and we were packed out most days. We had a good name for fresh fish and also mums individual steak and kidney pies and puddings which became legendary. Sausage and onion pies, homemade Scotch eggs. Thick club sandwiches, toasted sandwiches, Quiches, mum made it all. She always was a hard worker. My father too. People would drive over from nearby Haywards Heath and Burgess hill even came up from Brighton to eat with us.

Pub food like that was still quite rare in the 1970's. Most pubs did not serve food. You were lucky if you could get a ham sandwich or a ploughman's lunch. It would have been bread cheese and pickle but no salad. On the bar there would have been a big jar of pickled eggs. Disgusting tasting things they were. Crisps, peanuts and that was your lot in most pubs and only at lunchtime never at night.

Cuckfield was and is a very pretty village with some lovely property. Quintessentially English. 6 pubs then, small shops and tearooms.

Once the business had grown we had a good regular clientele. Mainly very nice people they were too. My mother was a great landlady, strict too. No swearing was allowed in the bar whatsoever. My dad was very placid and good natured and a charming landlord. My mum has a great sense of humour and is very kind, but she stood no nonsense. She was nicknamed Annie Walker after the landlady of the 'Rovers Return' in Coronation Street who also took no prisoners.

One night a few years later we had a 'Coronation Street' themed party night. My mother was Annie Walker of course, my dad Fred the cellar man and our barmaid Midge was Hilda Ogden. I was Bet Lynch. I'd been up to London to Tooting market and bought a replica of a blue polka dot dress that Bet wore a lot in the programme. I had the big blonde hair cigarette holder fish net tights high heels the works. We all stayed in character all night and refused to answer to any one unless the called us by our characters names. I had the voice off pat too. The customers loved it. Many of them dressed up as well and we were packed. It ended up with me on the piano in full drag playing all the old favourites and everyone singing at the top of their voices. For a joke before the party Mum and Dad went to Suffolk for a weeks break to see Aunt Nel, My Brother in law (Brian O'connor) and I for a joke got an estate agent to knock up a for sale board saying "sold to Annie Walker" The local paper the mid Sussex times featured me nailing it to the garage door. My parents nearly had heart failure when they got back and saw it. It was hilarious.

Aunty Pat had come down to join us from London. Mum got her a live in job working as warden at a home for retired ladies. She got free accommodation but no wage. She got taken on at a school for special needs children in the village as Cook. Like all my family Pat was a good cook and after working for the civil service had gone into catering too. However, she didn't last very long. One day she turned around from her stove to find a Down's syndrome boy masturbating furiously behind her. That was it she dropped her wooden spoon and walked straight out. She was so dramatic about it, I'm afraid I was in tears laughing when she told me later.

We were still very close. She came to work at the pub with us, which worked on some levels, depending on her moods or hangovers. We used to have lots of fun; I took her to the 42 club to meet my friend Terrie Varley which went well. We got her haircut in Brighton and she was mortified as it was so short she thought everyone would think she was a dyke. Aunt Nel who was staying with us nearly wet herself laughing when she saw her. Pat was so theatrical about everything. I took her and Aunt Nel to see our beloved Shirley Bassey in Brighton and included her in most things.

However, the time came when I met Colin and moved away. I don't think she ever really forgave me for this. Eventually her alcoholism took over and she was a bit of a nightmare. When mum and dad left the Talbot they left Pat in Cuckfield. We lost touch until she was dying from breast cancer and alcohol related problems years later. Mum and I went to see her on her death bed and all she asked for was a cigarette. I didn't give her one. I wish I had now. I still miss her she could be such fun. Her wishes were for no fuss and only the six of us attended her funeral. I had her coffin covered in white lilies. I picked Dorothy Squires singing 'Say it with flowers' as we went in and Judy Garland at Carnegie hall singing 'Over the rainbow' at the end. It really could not have been anything else.

12

FAMOUS FACES

Cuckfield being commutable to London and near Brighton had a lot of theatricals. Opposite us in Ockenden Lane lived the Fox family. Angela Fox the matriarch of the Fox acting dynasty. Her sons Edward and James were/still are both big film stars (The day of the Jackal, Edward and Mrs Simpson) James was in (The servant with Dirk Bogarde and Thoroughly modern Millie) Another son Robert is a top theatre producer. Angela was grandmother to Emila Fox, Laurence Fox and lots of other little foxes there are so many of them. They are legends in show business.

As Landlord of the Talbot my father inherited the title of the honorary Sheriff of Cuckfield. Cuckfield declared itself an Independent state years before and had its own passports and money. This was just a charity funding thing for fun. My Mother was elected as The Mayor of Cuckfield. She took her role seriously and raised an awful lot of money for local charities. She also introduced the Cuckoo Fayre, a summer fete that still exists to this day. On the grand opening she talked our local big star Edward fox to ride through the streets with her in a magnificent blue and gold Delaunay Belville veteran car with full police escorts in the annual Cuckfield pageant and parade, before arriving at the entrance to the park for the grand opening of the Cuckoo fayre. He was a big name at that time because of TV show Edward and Mrs Simpson and he drew huge crowds. The Cuckoo fayre was declared a wonderful Success. Mum worked hard that year but declined to do a second term as Mayor due to her already hectic workload.

Edwards Mother Angela was a regular customer of ours. A really lovely woman with a great smile, a twinkle in her eye and a good sense of humour. She used to bring lots of famous people who would stay with her, in for lunch. One day she introduced me to the great actress Judy Parfitt. She said Judy this is Jeremy, I call him the King of Cuckfield because all the girls love him. I went bright red.

It was not unusual to go down into the bar in the morning early lunchtime and see people like Ursula Howells a film star and famous then for a TV programme called 'Father dear Father' with Patrick Cargill. She and her husband Anthony Pelissier a film star and famous producer having an aperitif before lunch. Lots of colourful people. Even Lord Snowden Princess Margaret's husband who lived nearby in Staplefield would pop in for a drink pre lunch. He was great friends with Peter Jeeves who owned the antique shop next to the pub. Princess Margaret's children now Lord Linley and Lady Sarah Chatto used to play in our little car park (children under 14 were not allowed in pubs then whoever they were)

At Christmas my family were always special guests at Ockenden Manor. The beautiful Tudor manor house and hotel at the top of Ockenden Lane opposite the Talbot.

These were grand dinners, black tie and full evening dress. It was run by an old gay man with very flat feet called Douglas Wells. He was assisted by his extrovert manager Michael Kelly who was one of our best customers. At Christmas many stars and society people would book in for the festive season.

We would be invited up for dinner. I loved it. Drinks in the little bar before going into the most beautiful oak panelled dining room, beautifully laid with linen and silver and fresh flowers, with course after course of great food. A regular guest was Douglas Byng a very famous musical and revue star in the 1930s and 40's (Noel Coward used to be bottom of the bill starring Dougie billed as Little Master Coward). He was also famous for being a female impersonator.

After dinner he would get up and do an impromptu concert. He'd sing his old comedy songs. 'Miss Otis Regrets' (Cole Porter wrote it for me did you know?) 'Doris the Goddess of wind', 'I am a tree' and others. He had a very noticeable nervous tick and a stutter but strangely this disappeared when he was performing.

Other guests were Margaret The Duchess of Argyle who was rather notorious but good fun and the actress Irene Handel. Irene was very famous in British comedy films, hundreds of them. A national treasure she always played cockney women. In real life she was frightfully posh with Received Pronunciation and always with a little dog under her arm. A nice woman.

While Dougie Byng was staying at Ockenden Manor he would come down to the Talbot for drinks. He was a very tall man, very smartly dressed, topped off with a lovely velvet Cossack hat.

Camp as Christmas he liked me very much. In those days I wore quite a bit of jewellery as was fashionable at the time. He was always inviting me to his flat in Arundel Place in Kemp town Brighton for "tea" I was about 15 at the time but looked older. He'd say "Come to tea dear boy" (his head twitching with his nervous tic and stuttering) I shall know when you will be arriving, I shall see a flash of lightning from those diamonds all the way from St James street.

He made me laugh but I never went. I didn't really have much of a clue then about the gay scene then.

A few months later when I'd settled in a bit, a friend's sister Debbie got a job in the kitchen at Ockenden Manor and after school I would go there for afternoon tea. Sitting on the lawn or patio in my school uniform, with a pot of Earl grey tea and smoked salmon and cucumber sandwiches, cream cakes, all gratis of course. I learned to appreciate the finer things in life very early on.

13

A DARK PERIOD AN OUTSIDER

Jumping back, after the summer holidays of 1974 and settling into a new way of life, it was time for me to go to a new school. Warden Park was about 1/2 a mile away from the Talbot and I hated it.

I was an outsider from day one. A nice school and a good one it wasn't for me.

The first day after assembly which was led by the new headmaster a Mr Trethowan (who wore a teachers cape and mortar board hat which I found creepy) I was mobbed by a bunch of girls asking questions, who was I? Where was I from? One called Gill asked for a bit of my hair and comments such as "ooo he looks like David Essex." I looked nothing like him. I was so embarrassed. It didn't help that all the boys in my pier group witnessed what happened so they hated me from day one. Gill went on to be a bit of a stalker following me everywhere and turning up at classes I went to, every time I turned around this poor girl was there. I did try and befriend her but she was so besotted and agreed with everything I said so it was pointless.

I got through the day and the next one with bigger boys sidling up to me saying, "just because you're from London you think your special and you're not, we are going to get you after school" all that sort of bullying. I did not think I was special at all. I looked and sounded different. I had long wavy shoulder length hair and I had an earring, unusual then and my parents were mortified when I had had it done.

Then I spoke with a North London accent not cockney but London, different to these Home Counties types. I'd adapted this accent as a result of being laughed at when I went to Stag Lane Jr where I was considered Posh. My mother always made us speak properly, we didn't drop our T's or say ain't instead of not. Or say 'fick' instead of Thick. We just were not part of the fink and fought brigade at all. However, I roughed it up a bit to fit in.

Now I was in the reverse position. Eventually over time I did revert to my original Primrose Hill accent. Not Posh at all just "nicely" spoken.

I'd had this problem with girls before. I was a nice looking lad I suppose, a bit gawky like all teenagers. Once when I was about 11 years old my sister Deborah took me to see a friend of hers who was staying at an all girls camping site. When they saw me I got chased down the road with them yelling "Quick its Donny Osmond Its Donny Osmond" Dozens of girls running down the road after me waving bits of paper yelling DonnnnnEEE. My sister's boyfriend came after me in the car and they bundled me in. While I never looked like David Essex, I did look a tiny bit like Donny. We were a similar age and he was the number one heart throb at the time and topping the charts with Puppy Love. Now you're probably thinking I loved it but I didn't I hated it.

The next hurdle I had to cross was sports. I wouldn't do it. I had never done it at Chandos, well not since the age of 12. I used to get a letter from my mum or I'd write one myself and forge mums signature. I wrote letters for all my mates who didn't want to take part either. If it was a nice day we'd lay over the sport field sunbathing, smoking and listening to radio 1 on a transistor radio, otherwise we would sit in the library. It wasn't so much the sports I hated, although no fan of football even then, it was the communal undressing in front of all the other boys I hated. The thought of it used to give me nightmares literally. Also at Chandos we had two very peculiar gym teachers. I'll change their names. Mr Barry was an old man to us about 60, balding and a bit camp. He was a real weirdo in all ways. When we were first years aged 11 he'd stand at the end of the communal showers peering in at all the naked boys. As we came out he'd offer to dry our backs for us. He had a small room under the stairs with a camp bed in it. Where "special boys" were allowed to go and have a lie down if they felt tired. The older boys warned us, be careful of bum boy Barry, don't let him touch you or get too near. He was known throughout the school as bum boy Barry. Nothing was ever done about it. However as we got older we got our own back. He used to take chemistry as well and we gave him hell. Often reducing him to tears, served him right to. Paedophiles often work their way into these jobs, nobody spoke of such things then though.

The other one a Mr Skelling wasn't as blatant as Barry but he was always lurking around the changing rooms especially where the older more developed boys were. He made you shudder when you looked at him.

So I'm faced with this dilemma again at Warden Pk While the gym teacher there a Mr Revel wasn't a pervert he was a bully. We hated each other on sight. I refused to do sports, He tried to break me but he couldn't, which made him absolutely furious. Also it would have been a good chance for the bullies there to get me on the sport field and give me a good kicking. I had never been a fighter. I've always had a big mouth though and could use it to withering effect even then. I started to get called a poof again and all the name calling. I had no inclination then I was gay, quite the opposite in fact, but I must have given off something they could sense. Anyway I carried on writing the notes with various ailments. I was made to go to doctors and be examined all sorts. I wouldn't give in.

The bullying, the teachers not understanding me, homesickness for London missing my friends all caused me to become ill with nerves and stress. I started getting really bad stomach pains and refused to go to school I had a bit of a breakdown.

My mother would make me go to the local doctor every single day. "If you are ill get yourself up the doctors" eventually and unbelievably the doctor gave me stomach medicine and prescribed Librium a strong tranquilliser.

This made me feel very ill so after a few weeks he put me onto Valium. This started a long life of taking prescription drugs like these and various 'mood changers' Unforgivable I think now giving tranquillisers to a 14 year old.

Of course the time came when I had to go back to school, but the only way they could get me there was by car right up to the headmaster's office outside door and a valium.

My father had by now ditched the old Morris Minor and bought a beautiful Mercedes. I'd sweep up the drive in this causing more resentment. Once I went through the headmasters entrance I'd wave my dad goodbye and leg it out of the back door and over the fields, where I'd walk until lunchtime, go home for lunch and then pretend I was going back, but instead I would go back to the woods and hide. I got through this awful period by looking forward to the weekend.

On Friday nights I'd go home get changed, pack a bag, collect my £5 a week pocket money, catch the bus to Haywards Heath train station and go back to London.

At Victoria I'd make my way to my dear friend Carol Bonds house via tube trains and buses to Wealdstone in Harrow, it was quite a journey, but I did it every week for a long time. My parents didn't mind, they knew how unhappy I was and that I was safe at Carols. Her family mum, dad, two sisters and brother made me very welcome. They were totally laid back and used to let us have the front room to smoke, play records, a few drinks. By now we had progressed to Gin and Bacardi and Coke and have our friends come round. Carol was 2 years older than me 16, but most of my friends were older. This place was a sanctuary for me then and I'm eternally grateful to Carol and her family. I'm still in touch with Carol to this day. Thank you Carol.

My Stomach would churn going back to Cuckfield on Sunday evenings.

14 is not a good age to move to a new area for children.

My parents needed to do it and I understand it. In fact I bene-fited enormously in some ways, it opened my mind up and made me far more sophisticated in a worldly sense than if I'd have stayed in Edgware, but it was hell at the beginning.

Juliette Harris, Barr, Me on my 21st, Chipmunk. Talbot Pub

Dad with new Mercedes, Me aged 14

Kim Cusden first love

Kim Prowen my protector!

Me about 16

Margot, Keith, Cynthia and me at the Talbot Inn

Me and Kim at the bar Ockenden
manor aged 15 so 1975

Me as Shirley Bassey

Me as Bet Lynch coronations street night

Mum as mayor of cuckfield   My Xmas Card 1978

Pat me John Nellie Shirley Bassey outing

Jeremy Goodchild and the convincing sign put up outside the Talbot Inn to welcome his parents home

Joke just up their street

Diane and Don Goodchild returned to their home at The Talbot Inn, Cuckfield, on Saturday night, after a holiday in Suffolk, hoping for a quiet, relaxing weekend. But to their horror, as their car pulled into the drive, they saw a "Sold" sign on the verge done.

Gasps of disbelief gave way to howls of laughter as Diane and Don looked more closely at the sign, for it read "Sold to Annie Walker," whom they recognised as the licensee of the Rover's Return, the pub from the television programme, Coronation Street.

The convincing sign was

provided by Mr. John Duffy, a regular at the Talbot, and was put up by the Goodchild's son, Jeremy, and a friend, Brian Connor.

Diane, who is "Mayor" of Cuckfield, explained: "When we go on holiday the regulars get up to some trick or other. Last year they put a sign up in the bar saying 'under new management.' It took us a long time to convince customers that we were not going. Even now people ask us if we really have sold the pub, and some even ask who Annie Walker is."

This year the joke is two-sided, for on Saturday evening the

Goodchilds are organising a television night to raise money for the Independent State of Cuckfield.

Licensees and customers will dress up as television personalities, and Diane has a choice as to who she will be! Don will be Fred Gee, and assistant Midge will be Hilda Ogden, with Jeremy as the buxom blond Bet Lynch.

People visiting the Talbot on Saturday night, who see the "Sold" sign and are served by familiar Coronation Street characters might wonder if the imaginary world has suddenly become real.

For charity

Pageant of colour in 'UDI' gala

Pictured above, the Mayor of Cuckfield and Mrs Goodchild, drink a glass of champagne outside The Talbot

A bottle of good cheer for Cuckfield charities was cracked open last Saturday by the "Mayor" of the Independent State of Cuckfield, Mrs Diane Goodchild—and a total of £13A41J was totted up. Our picture shows Mrs. Goodchild, in her mayoral robes, about to crack the bottle held by her husband, Don, landlord of the Talbot Inn. Surrounding them are some of the generous customers, who helped fill the bottle with cash during the past six months. Mrs. Goodchild has been "Mayor" of the "Independent State" for a year, and has sponsored many other schemes to raise funds to be distributed to local charities

The Mayor of Cuckfield and Edward Fox

The first Cuckoo Fayre is 'fantastic'

The Talbot Inn Cuckfield

With family and Friends Inn on the park Park lane. London.

With Jane Prior at the Talbot aged 14

With Nellie in Dieppe

14

ADAPTING

Eventually I took the ball by the horns and returned to school. I never did do sports. I coped with the bullies by using my mouth and some of my older London friends and Kim of course with Debbie in tow, would skip school or bunk off as we used to say, or have a day off work and catch the train down to Haywards Heath and stand outside the school gates to meet me. If anyone had a go at me I'd say wait till you see what I've got lined up for you after school. Once they saw my London buddies older much harder and threatening it stopped. I'd point out the main culprits and my gang would have a word.

This gave me the reputation for being someone not to mess with but it didn't endear me to anyone either particularly. I did make two male friends Glen and Paul who both turned out to be gay when they were older, Glen it was obvious with but not with Paul and I so much. There was as always a group of girls around me and they were my safety net these people.

Keeping me sane as well were my two dear friends from Primrose Hill now living in Hove the twins Jane and Karen Prior. Jane had been my girlfriend for a while and she and Karen would come over to Cuckfield or I'd go and meet them in Brighton and go to concerts. Our hero Jimmy Ruffin came to the Brighton Dome. We got tickets and smuggled a bottle of gin watered down with lime under our coats and 20 fags of course and went to listen to Jimmy sing all his wonderful hits. 'What becomes of the brokenhearted' and our favourite 'Farewell is a lonely sound'. After the show, emboldened by the gin no doubt we jumped up onto the stage. His No1 dressing room was on the stage behind the curtain. There was a big grand piano still on stage and I sat down and started playing 'Farewell is a lonely sound' while the girls sang. Anyway Jimmy Ruffin stuck his head out of the door to see what all the racket was. He laughed and invited us into his dressing room where he signed autographs for us all and chatted away. He was a very nice man. Incredibly tall and I think one of Tamla Motown's greatest singers.

My new friend Glen introduced me to a lovely girl called Kim who was to become my regular girlfriend, so it wasn't all gloom and things were definitely looking up on the social side.

My form teacher at Warden Park was the music teacher and I was hoping I'd get involved with all that again but he was useless and lazy. A Mr Wolf, he'd say at music class, "I've got a lot of books to mark today so come on Goodchild get on the piano and get the class to have a sing song" That was it, nothing else.

So my mother got me private lessons again so I could continue to take my grade 5 piano exam. However my teacher who was very nice was only a young girl really and she said "to be honest Jeremy you can play better than I can, so why am I teaching you? Get someone else" I didn't and it was a shame looking back. I would have liked to have got up to grade 8 which is the top. Still I always had the ability to play and earned money when I needed it later on.

I'd like to say I became a star pupil but I didn't. I was angry, resentful, had a bad attitude, a typical teenager. I was cheeky to all the teachers and sometimes got the other kids in trouble. I'd pinch bottles of Pils lagers from the cellar and smuggle them and more into school. At lunchtimes we'd get a bit drunk and try to recreate the parties I used to have at Pandy's house in London. It wasn't the same. I didn't really learn much. I always enjoyed English and got stuck into that and eventually got an O'level but nothing else. I was threatened with expulsion 3 times, my parents were always getting called up to the school with complaints from teachers and other parents about my behaviour and they would calm it down with a cheque for the school fund or a case of sherry for the raffle. Once I nearly didn't make it because I'd had a row with Mr Wolf, he went for me and I punched him in the mouth.

Once I was called into the office of the deputy head a vicious old dyke called Miss Mac. While I stood there she said to these worried parents. "The trouble with Goodchild (I always absolutely hated being called by my surname) is he's not really a bad boy but he's not a child, he's a boy with an adult brain" actually she had summed me up perfectly.

My house master known by the girls as bra pinger Basil for obvious reasons said "why don't you get more involved"? I said in what? He said "well we've got a three legged race coming up next week you could join in that." I looked at him with utter contempt and incredulity and said, If you think I'm going to tie my leg to some idiot and try and run around the playground making myself look a total Pratt you've got another thing coming. He gave up after that.

On my last day Mr Revel the gym teacher came up to me and putting his face right up to mine snarling said. "You wait you little shit you'll make nothing of your life, you'll be nothing, no one." I replied watch me, and while you're at it take this school and shove it right up your fucking arse you............ and walked straight out of the headmasters entrance, never to return.

In hindsight if I had of started at this school at aged 11 like the others I would have done very well, at 14 everyone's made their friends settled in etc. It wasn't the schools fault.

I must say that the headmaster there Mr Trethowan who everyone was terrified of, was always very kind to me. I'd sit down in his office and have a chat; he spoke to me as an adult not a silly child. I'm not sure he understood the full extent of my unhappiness, I never told anyone about the bullying or my complete dread of getting naked in front of other boys, but he tried to understand and knew deep down I wasn't bad but that I didn't quite fit in.

15

I'LL SHOW THEM!

The very next day after leaving school aged 15 not quite 16, With Mr Revel's insults ringing in my ears, I caught an early train up to London to find a job. I'd decided to become a Chef. I was good at cooking. I'd also by now had quite a lot of experience helping out in the pub at home.

I walked from Victoria up to Park Lane and started what turned out to be a long day. I went in every hotel in Park Lane and asked for a job as a commis chef. I'd walk straight up to the desk suited and booted and ask to see the manager. I saw lots of them, mostly it was sorry we don't need anyone, or you're a bit young. However I still have a letter from the manager of the Hilton hotel in Park Lane who was so impressed with my enthusiasm and boldness he said, go and get two years training and then come back and bring this letter with you and I'll give you a job.

However this didn't help my immediate situation. I'd figured, go to all the best places and ask. If you want to learn a craft go to the top. I eventually made my way to Claridge's and was sent around the back of the hotel a bit like a servants entrance and told to ask there at the employment desk. When I got there I asked again and was met with "you're too young and you're not a union member." I said '"I've just left school I haven't had a job yet how can I be a union member"? "Sorry son to work here you've got to be a member of a trade union". 'Ok I'll join what do I have to do'? "To be in a trade union son you have to have a job" That's what it was like terrible. Actors had the same problem getting an equity card.

It wasn't just Claridge's either I got this in several hotels. In the 1970's the unions controlled everything. They were awful. They were always going on strike over any little thing. We had 3 day weeks. Where people could only go to work for 3 days, power cuts where we sat in the dark and lit candles every night for a few hours. They brought the country to its knees and by 1979 under Labours Jim Callaghan's watch we had the "winter of discontent" when things ground to a halt and they wouldn't even bury the dead. There were coffins piled up in the streets in some areas. It was cold and we had no heat because the miners were on strike again. This is how a certain Margaret Thatcher came to power. She single handedly fought back and smashed the unions reducing they're iron fist hold of the country and stopped their blackmail. It was ugly but it worked and she saved the country. I know not everyone sees it like that, but having lived throughout that era that's my opinion. The 1970's were a dark period in British history.

Another terrible thing we had to endure were the terrorist bombs from the IRA. You never knew when they would attack, my sister Deborah just missed getting blown up in the Harrods bomb. Then there was the Brighton Bomb where they tried to murder Margaret Thatcher they didn't get her but others were terribly injured. One of the saddest was when they blew up Lord Louis Mountbatten Uncle of Prince Phillip. Murdered along with two others in a boat in Ireland.

I remember this had an effect on us all. There was a sense of national grief. I caught the train up to London on my own and stood outside Westminster Abbey with thousands of others for the funeral to pay my respects. I remember Prince Charles walking along with Mountbatten's horse Dolly with Mountbatten's riding boots turned back to front in the stirrups. It was a moving sight, and a surprisingly short Prince Charles was visibly moved. Next came the Queen riding in the Royal car with the Queen Mother. The Queen

Mother was smiling and doing the royal wave at the crowds as they drove slowly by and I saw the Queen nudge her mother and say Mummy stop it! Vera Lynn was also there. We listened to the service outside on speakers. The atmosphere was very calm and quiet despite there being police with machine guns posted all around us on the roofs.

Anyway I digress; eventually somebody suggested I go to the Chef centre in Soho to a job agency. So tired and a bit fed up I made my way by foot up to Soho and found the Chef centre. I went in, filled out the forms and eureka I got an interview for a job. The trouble was it was at the Old Ship Hotel...... In Brighton!. It was a well know hotel but I'd dreamt of working in the West End but it was impossible with me not being a union member apparently. So I said yes and they arranged an interview for me with the head Chef called Pat Saywer for the next day. I got the job at £14 a week to train as a commis Chef I started the next Monday.

Despite my terrible last years of school and despite that horrible teacher telling me I'd never get anywhere, I was the first person in my year that year to get a job and I'm very proud of that.

16

LOVE AND ROMANCE

About 18 months or so before I left school. As I mentioned before I had made friends with two Cuckfield Boys Glen and Paul. Paul was from London like me and had also joined at the same time, so we were in similar situations. Glen was Cuckfield born and bred. He was great friends with a girl called Kim who lived opposite the pub in Ockenden lane above an art gallery. The artist a Mr Beauguard specialising in modern art lived above with his daughter Colette known to everyone as Barr and two elder step children Kim Cusden and the older brother Danny.

It was an unusual set up but seemed to work. Mr B used to go up to London every Saturday to sell his art work at Hyde Park. He would stay overnight and come back home on Sunday evening. Leaving the children aged then approximately 12, 14+ & 15+ to fend for themselves which they were quite capable of.

I used to see this beautiful tall blonde girl around the village and wondered who she was. Eventually Glen introduced us. Up close she was even more beautiful. 5ft 11 inches tall, a true blonde with huge big blue eyes. She was very slim and she looked a lot like a young Princess Diana. It didn't take long, probably two weeks at the most and we were in love and an item. My innocent teenage romance with Jane and crush on the other Kim had fizzled out like they do. We stayed friends. There had been a couple of girlfriends but nothing serious, although one girl about three years older than me had picked me to take her virginity, she asked if I'd oblige which I did on the floor in the sitting room above the bar in the Talbot. It wasn't romantic at all but who would have said no?

Soon Kim and I were lovers but we were very sensible. She was a virgin and went to see the doctor and had a chat and the doctor put her on the pill.

This was for both of us our first true love affair. It was very sweet, lots of fun and very loving and romantic.

I was the same height I looked older than my years and so did Kim, we made an attractive couple and were together every minute we could be. The visits to London became less now. Carol and our friend Paul Ledster who had a car would drive down and occasionally stay with Kim and I and family minus dad above the art gallery. Other friends too, most of the London crew at different times.

The massive studio above the art gallery was now party central on Saturday nights. Kim had a good part time job in a newsagents. So we were never short of cigarettes. I worked in the pub helping in the kitchen and doing odd jobs washing glasses etc. So we had a bit of cash. When we could afford it we would catch the train into Brighton or go dancing in the Disco called Cinderella's a good taxi ride away. You were supposed to be 18 of course but we all easily passed and we'd go and strut our stuff to Candy Statton's 'Young hearts run free' This of course was the peak of disco. For us Cinderella's was really cool, it wasn't really but for us it was heaven. If we couldn't afford it we would have a whip round and I would go up to the off licence and buy some booze for a party.

My mother wouldn't have approved of me staying over, So I'd go home about midnight as mum and dad were going to bed, I'd wait for them to fall asleep and then nip out again, jumping over the stable doors we had in the catering kitchen. I'd run back over the road and continue with the party, or jump into bed with Kim and then creep back in the morning, what fun.

Kim and I remained an item for close on two years. We even got secretly engaged, my parents would have been thrilled if we were older. They adored Kim. Eventually with a bit of financial help and encouragement from my mother, Kim went to a beauty and model school. She went on to become a successful model and even appeared in Vogue. She eventually married a successful Brighton Restaurateur and both of them were at my 21st birthday party at The Talbot a few years later. We are not in touch now sadly.

Towards the end of my relationship with Kim there was a boy started coming in the pub who was a lot of fun. To my horror I developed a huge crush on him, I couldn't understand it. There had been the odd twinge when I saw a good looking actor on TV before but nothing much. I'd buried it very deep I expect. Anyway nothing came of it because he was straight, so was I, I thought.

17

STARTING WORK

Stomach churning I left home about 7. 30am either to catch a bus or dad would run me or Deborah to the station, get on an early train about 8am to be at work at the Old Ship Hotel in Brighton for 9am. I was usually early so stopped in this little cafe in the Lanes. (A famous area of Brighton, pedestrianised and winding alleys with shops and restaurants) This cafe was called the Lorelli run by two gay chaps. It was a popular place to stop for coffee or lunch and quite a famous gay meeting place in the 1970's although I didn't know that then.

I walked down Ship Street and through the staff entrance, was directed to the staff changing room and horror of horrors was given a locker and told to get changed, in front of others. I don't know why I had this fear, all I can think of was that deep down in my subconscious there was a gay man lurking and maybe that's why I always felt a bit different and was shy of undressing in front of other men. Who knows?

So I found the lock up toilet and got changed into my brand new chefs uniform complete with hideous hat and emerged from there and put my clothes in the locker. Nobody noticed. I walked towards the main kitchens clutching my gleaming set of recently purchased knives to find Pat the head Chef. I had been up to Soho in London to be fitted out with two sets of everything. Cost my folks a pretty penny, but you had to have it.

Talk about arrive in another world! Did I get my eyes opened. I was put to work with a nice enough Chef named Stan in his late 50's I suppose. Remember I wasn't quite 16 then. It was a terrifying atmosphere, Noisy, manic and the swearing! It was a bit like being in an army barracks.

I was helping out on vegetables first. I had to cook Salsify I'd never heard of it. Big batches had to be prepared for that days Lunch. It was served with a béchamel sauce (white sauce) I already knew how to make this as my mother had taught me how to make it and onion sauce when I was about 7. However, not in the huge quantities we had to make there. There was creamed spinach to cook, glazed carrots and much more. Everything then was based on French Cuisine.

I quite enjoyed it and after a few days had settled into my department well enough. We had a break after lunch at 2.30pm until 6pm when we had to return to the hotel for the dinner service. We worked until about 9.30pm and then went home. This was awkward for me. Because Cuckfield was a train ride away it was too far to go home in the afternoon break, so I found myself wandering around the shops in all weathers. After a few months of this I was moaning about it to one of the Chefs, a nice guy called Larry. Larry was one of the friendlier ones, Pat the head chef was nice too but most of them were miserable gruff buggers. He said in his Northern Irish accent, You don't want to be doing that, come with me and some of the lads, (from various departments in the hotel,) I'll take you up to the 42 club, I said what's that, he said an afternoon private drinking club around the corner. So I did and this was a life changing moment for me.

18

THE 42 CLUB

Situated on the sea front in Brighton above a rock shop was the 42 Club. It was the first gay club in Brighton. Behind the rock shop display stands, outside the rock shop was a door; you pushed the intercom button and waited for a woman with a strong northern accent to say "who is it? okay open the door lurve" Up two flights of stairs and a lady behind a serving hatch to the bar had a good look at you, and if she approved, released the catch and let you into the bar entrance. All a bit cloak and dagger but it was members and guests only. There were lots of afternoon drinking clubs in Brighton and London in those days because all the pubs had to shut by law at 2.30-3pm. If you didn't live in an area like Brighton you had to wait until 6pm when the pubs reopened if you wanted a drink.

I walked into this glamorous club with Larry feeling very excited inside. Behind the bar was this vision, a good looking woman in her 50's with a high piled up hairstyle with a bun at the top, but through the middle wound a white streak. A bit like Cruella de Ville. This was Terrie Varley the manager.

The club was owned by ex dancer Tony Stuart and artist Syd Lewis. They did the night shift and Terrie did the afternoon shift. She had been there for years and was apparently a bit of a legend on the Brighton club and gay scene.

She ran the club with a rod of iron and a mouth like a drunken sailor. She was also very kind and extremely funny. From St Helens in Lancashire she had always dreamt of escaping the north and settling in Brighton. She did with the first man in her life. There were a couple of others, not many. She had two children that we knew of, one called Susan who was in a home for the mentally ill and another very pretty girl called Clarrissa.

Terrie had a very hard life and struggled to make ends meet. She worked hard all her life but it wasn't really very easy for Clarrissa. The only work Terrie, now a single mother could get was bar work, cleaning and waitressing. However by the time I met her she was on her feet, doing well at the 42 club and rented a large house in Over street with 4 bedrooms where she did bed and breakfast for gay men visiting Brighton.

She was known for her "catch phrases like "open the door lurve" and if anyone offered her a drink she'd say "thanks lurve I'll have 20ps worth.... I might as well get pissed then fooked darlin, no chance of that, not in 'ere anyway cheers" She always said it and it always made people laugh. She swore like a trooper, but she could get away with it, some people can. She had comic timing.

Although she was not every ones cup of tea. She said exactly what she thought good or bad and she could be quite rude. If you were not used to her she could cause offence on occasion. Not that it worried her "fook em lurve pair of cunts" was the usual retort. (cunt was pronounced Coont)

One day this man said to her "Terrie what's wrong with me? No one seems to like me I wonder why"

Terrie trying her best to be sympathetic said "there's nothing wrong with you darlin, nothing at all, (pause) you're just a bit of a "coont" that's all lurve"

The poor guy was ashen faced as she walked away to insult another.

Once years later, she was staying at a hotel in Benidorm, Colin and I went to meet her. She was laying around the pool on a sunbed. When we approached her she said at the top of her voice "hello love, alright? Take a look around you; go on look, now then, have you ever seen so many ugly fat fuckers in all of yer life eh?" We were mortified; the looks from the other holiday makers were incredulous. She wasn't being rude in her mind she was just telling the truth, which she was. Also we didn't realise then but dementia was taking hold of her.

I was Lucky, Terrie liked me very much. We became friends from that first day of meeting each other until the day she died many years later. She was one of the best friends I ever had. She protected me when I was 16 and always stood up for me. I also looked after her the best I could. She considered me the son she never had. Our friendship lasted over 30 years and we loved each other.

The 42 club then was a cosy one room bar with a little dance floor and a juke box at one end and a picture window at the front with a sea view. There was a large bar and barstools to sit at with a curve at one end, and various chairs and tables dotted about. It was well decorated by Syd whose camp touch made it a very comfortable place to spend the afternoons. Although a gay club lots of straight people used it too in the afternoons. Gangsters and club owners from London down for the races, other publicans having a break in the afternoon, chefs and waiters like us, pretty boys, old Queens and few lesbians a real mix. Everyone got on and it didn't matter what your sexual preference was, nobody cared. Brighton was like that even then. There was also a good smattering of theatricals, who may be appearing at the Theatre Royal or the Dome.

It wasn't unusual in the early days for Dorothy Squires (big singing star and wife of James Bond actor Roger Moore) to pop in for a drink. She used to stay with her sister in law in Hove Joyce Goulding who was Tony Stuart the owner's old dancing partner in variety. Joyce lived in Hove with Dorothy's niece Emily.

Also Ann Todd the film star used to pop in with Vivienne Leigh (Scarlet O'Hara), then married to Sir Laurence Olivier, Russ Conway the famous pianist, Danny La Rue, all sorts. One regular was Joan Turner a famous comedienne with a very good operatic voice. She was often teamed with closet gay comic Jimmy Edwards, who was also a customer.

Joan Turner was not a very nice person. She would appear at the bar swathed in furs, some of the boys fawned over her. If anyone asked her to have a drink it was always "I'll have a bottle of champagne darling thank you" She got away with this on several occasions.

In the end Terrie got fed up with her and told her "Fuck off you fucking old ponce. Get your arse out of here and don't come back. You're not going to upset my customers, now out! And don't come back, do you hear me?"

You can't speak to me like that I'm Joan Turner.

"I don't give a 'fook' who you are 'darlin' OUT."

She got a round of applause for that.

One day for a laugh, one of the regulars Alan Cheisman said to me watch this, I'm just popping round to the phone box to play a joke on Varley. Now it was quite busy this day and Terrie was a bit run off of her feet, anyway the phone kept ringing and ringing while she was serving. Eventually she stopped, turned the music down and said "Hello 42 Club, who is it? Who is it you want? I don't know him darlin, hang on ill ask" At the top of her voice she yelled out in pure Lancashire. "Oy as anyone in ere seen Mike Hunt?" which came out as "MY Coont" Silence then, "No and we don't fucking want to thanks very much" was the reply from the customers. Well, when she realised she had been had she collapsed in hysterics as did all the people in the bar.

People were crying with laughter. It really was funny and Terrie could always take a joke.

Although one day I got there early and she wasn't happy at all! "You'll never fuckin believe it Jeremy we've been burgled, I've had the police ere. The bastard got through the back door up the fire escape. And you'll never believe what the dirty coont did! Me horrified said what? "They only went and took a shit in me new ice bucket lurve! The dirty fookin bastard!" I had to turn my head as she rinsed it out under the tap.

Over the next 20 years I would spend a lot of my time with Terrie Varley at the 42 club, on and off.

19

Enjoying Brighton life

We didn't drink too much at the 42 club if we were going back to work at the Old Ship Hotel for the dinner shift. Just a few beers, but some did.

The hotel made a big mistake by hiring kitchen porters to do the washing up and cleaning on a daily basis.

These down and out type rough sleepers would queue outside the staff entrance every morning to be taken on for the day. They were fine at the lunch time session. But they used to pay them after lunch. By the time we all came back on duty about 5.30-6pm they were legless and fighting and shouting with each other. Sometimes you'd have to duck as a plate came flying through the air. The Chef would throw them out but most got taken on again the next day.

Also there was an old lady known as big Rose in the still room, if she had too many gins in the break she could be a right cow.

God help the waiters who asked for more melba toast. She would chuck the bread at them and say make it your fucking self.

I made lots of friends at the old ship. They were a colourful bunch, a mixed bag. I had got my friend from Cuckfield Paul, a job as a waiter and an old friend from London Martin one too. They both earned far more than my £14 a week as they got tips as well. £14 a week was dreadful money even then, you could get £20-30 pw for working in a shop just serving. However I was learning a trade supposedly so you accepted the low wage. Always thought it unfair though that the kitchen never got a share of the tips. Without nice food the waiters wouldn't have got tipped would they?

We made good friends with Angie a tall black girl. Very beautiful striking looks. She wore fantastic turbans and was the head housekeeper and resembled Grace Jones who had a massive hit at the time with 'La vien rose' Luckily she didn't share Grace's temperament and was like a big sister to us all.

Also there were two brothers from Scotland (well they were 1/2 brothers) great guys but the fact they were lovers too and both had girlfriends took some getting the head around I can tell you.

They all started coming up the 42 club as well and at night we would go to night clubs in Brighton. Punk was just starting, but there was also a very good soul bar/club called originally 'The Inn place" on the seafront where I used to go with Angie. One of the pubs we used was 'The Belvedere' under the arches on Brighton beach it had a late licence. It was also a "brothel" I used to be able to subsidise my £14 p/w income by playing the piano in there. The landlady/Madam liked me and would give me big tips to play the country and western song 'little old wine drinker me' for her. My friends also got free drinks like me. At the end of the night the girls (prostitutes) would hand around the hat and put money in for me. They were lovely and always very generous. I would often get more than my week's wages in a couple of hours. This was the first time I could use my piano playing to earn money, but not the last.

I was still with Kim my girlfriend then and the Cuckfield friends came along too on occasions.

Being in Brighton meant you always knew what was going on. We would sit in the newly opened Browns restaurant with a coffee and a plate of something to share and listen to a new singer called Bette Midler. Another Bette was coming to town to a certain Miss Bette Davis. I was a huge fan, (so should have guessed something was up then) she was bringing her one woman show to the Theatre Royal and I got tickets. Talk about exciting. For the first 30 minutes the sold out theatre watched clips from her old movies like Now voyager "why ask for the moon we have the stars" All about Eve "fasten your seat belts it's gonna be a bumpy night" and then she walked on stage. The audience went mad. The standing ovation and cheering went on for probably 10 minutes. People were in tears including me. When it went quiet she said "What a dump" another of her catch phrases and minced across the stage with her famous walk, cigarette in hand large puffs of smoke, a glass of scotch on the table and answered questions from the audience for another hour and more. It was a magical evening and I'll never forget it.

Not long after the other Bette would come to town The Divine miss M, Bette Midler. She was at the Dome with her outrageous act she did in a wheelchair dressed as a mermaid. We all went of course and she was fantastic. On stage for over 2 hours nonstop. What a performer. After that she did the Palladium and TV shows and became a super star in every field.

After being at the old ship for nearly a year I asked the head chef if and when I would ever start my day release at Brighton College. I should have started months before but it always got left. Anyway this time he got things going and I started at the new term. I'm afraid I hated it. It was just like being back at school. The teacher was another bully who shouted at people like they were dirt, seemed to be permanently angry with everyone and it was like history repeating itself. I stopped going and took the day off to do other things. Eventually the head chef Pat said, I hear you've been bunking off going to college why? I told him I hated it, that after working in the hotel for a year I didn't want to go back to that school boy atmosphere, he was sympathetic and understood but said you'll have to go Jeremy the hotel have paid for the course. I tried for a bit longer but hated it. With a different teacher I would have stuck it out. Plus at the hotel I wasn't learning the craft as I thought I should be.

Catering in the 1970's was a different entity then it is now. Starters at The Old Ship could consist of literally a glass of to-mato juice, A Florida cocktail, (tinned mandarins and grapefruit segments), a plate of wilted lettuce and tomato was a mixed salad no dressing or of course a prawn cocktail.

The food if I'm honest wasn't very good at The Old Ship. Hotel food then often wasn't.

I was moved into the fish department for a while to do the wilted salads (for some reason prepared in the fish room, cool I suppose) I improved them a lot and got lots of compliments from the other chefs and I had to fillet the fish and breadcrumb it etc to send it out to the main kitchen for cooking.

One day somebody bought in two polystyrene boxes and put them on the work bench behind me. I was busy chopping away when all of sudden these boxes started to move. Looking out of the corner of my eye I thought I was seeing things. Then there was a big lurch as the boxes jumped into the air. I was petrified. I ran over to the intercom on the wall and pushed the button and yelled for help. Pretty soon some of the chefs were rushing in to see what all the fuss was about.

When I told them they started to piss themselves with laughter. Apparently in the boxes were live lobsters. I didn't know and I thought they were sending me up when they told me I'd have to boil them alive to cook them. They weren't, you could hear them scream as they tried to get out of the pot that had a lid on with a big wooden spoon through it attached to the handles so they couldn't get out. I refused to do it and got Larry or one of the others to do it.

We used to get busy around the conference season. We would have the trade unions first. Everyone dreaded it as it was always a nightmare. Vic Feather was the big union boss back then. He used to keep the restaurant open way past closing time so none of us would get home on time. Smoke a big fat cigar and click his fingers at the waiters. An utter pig. The waiters used to spit in his food before it went out.

After that would be the Labour party and then the Conservatives.

Neither were any bother. The Conservatives being the most considerate on the time factor so we could leave on time and good tippers. The only difference was there was one price for the Labour party and another for the Conservatives.

One night I had an order for Dover Sole it was the same sole that had been hanging around since the Labour conference the week before, just a few pounds more on the menu. It was a bit smelly and I went to chuck it but was yelled at and told to scrub it under the sink in cold water and salt.

So what with the day release nightmare at college and the general malaise and disillusionment that had set in, in the Hotel generally I handed in my notice. The head chef tried to persuade me to stay as did a couple of the others but I didn't feel I was learning enough and was being used for cheap labour. My wages only covered my fares and I still had to rely on a top up allowance from my Parents. I was a bit resentful of having to work such long hours for such a small wage when people on the dole seemed to be getting more than me.

20

MY GAP YEAR

I took off to my Uncle Tony's Pub up on the Norfolk Broads for a few weeks holiday on my Own. Kim was still at school I think. It was a lovely place The Ferry boat Inn in Surlingham.

I had a change of scene and mucked in helping in the bar and kitchen. It was a seasonal pub, packed in the summer empty in the winter.

After a few weeks I went back to Cuckfield and worked in the Talbot until I found another job.

I went back down to Brighton to see my friends. I couldn't believe the changes that had happened in just a few weeks.

I located my Friend Paul working in a gay pub called 'The New Heart and Hand' on the seafront in Brighton. He'd had enough of the old ship too. Martin our other friend had stayed there and eventually was dragged home by his parents who thought we were a bad influence.

I walked into this vast pub. 4 bars, 3 were gay and there was a straight nightclub underneath. Paul was behind the bar wearing what looked like eye makeup. I said what the fuck are you doing working in here? He said "I'm gay dear, I've come out, I like men dear not girls" I said stop calling me dear. He was camping about behind the bar calling the customers dear and love. This shy boy had turned into Bet Lynch over night.

Anyway he said wait until I finish work and I'll take you to the

Curtain club. I said I'm not going down there it's full of poufs. Oh give it a chance said Paul it's a really nice club you'll love it dear!

Anyway after him slipping me free drinks for a couple of hours I agreed to go.

Down some dodgy steps underneath the Queens Hotel on the seafront was The Curtain Club. You rang on the door and a man called Andy opened the door very smartly dressed in a cream suit, black shirt and tie. He had grey hair and very blue eyes and looked a bit like Steve Mcqueen. He said "Hello Paul, then looking at me he said to Paul, whose this you've picked up then" I looked him straight in the eye and said don't be so familiar your only the door-man. He roared with laughter, he said "I hope your 21?" me, "of course I am"

We were 16-17. We didn't have to pay. It turned out us young ones got in free to attract the older men who spent. I had a great night, after I got over the initial shock of seeing so many men all ages in one place, some dancing together, some kissing I was ok. Paul introduced me to a few guys who seemed very nice. There was a great atmosphere. There was no threat of violence unlike in the straight discos and pubs. Lots of laughing. The music was great bang up to date with the coolest Dj's in town. I got bought lots of drinks.

The Curtain club was made up of three bars, a quietish one in the front for conversation and a juke box. A side middle bar which was more cruisy but another comfortable lounge bar. All well decorated and furnished, it was not a dump by any means, and then at the end a disco bar for dancing with a smallish dance floor.

The club was owned by 3 guys Peter (Wendy) Brown, Michael Platt and his partner Derek. They had great staff. Handsome Don on the front bar, Chinese Tony in the middle and Dragonella (Tony) on the disco bar. Dragonella lived on vodka and water and didn't eat much I remember.

So as you can gather I became quite a regular. Soon I was taking Kim and Barr down and some of the other Cuckfield gang. We got in because Andy the door man fancied me. It was very cool to be bisexual in the 1970's even if you were not. The new romantic thing was just starting. We were hip had the latest clothes and lived for music, drinking and dancing. The big hits I remember of that time played constantly at the Curtain Club were 'Cherchez La Femme' by Dr Buzzards original Savannah Band, Thelma Houston's 'Don't leave me this way' and Yvonne Fair 'It should have been me' Words like gender fluid hadn't been thought of. People were either camp or not. I was not I was straight acting and had a girlfriend so I was a challenge.

By now of course I was curious and one night after weeks of chatting me up I went back to Andy's house with him. This was taking a risk he was 42 and I was only about 16 ish It was illegal then for two men to sleep together unless they were 21 and then they had to be alone in private, and the older one would have gone to prison if caught.

The next morning I woke up and I felt a sense of relief. Happiness almost. Nothing had felt wrong or weird and I realised that something I had unconsciously suppressed in myself so deeply had come to the fore.

I couldn't tell anyone except Paul and carried on as normal. I saw Andy lots more over the next few weeks and we fell in love. So eventually I had to break the news to Kim. She cried but was very sweet and understanding. We still slept together occasionally afterwards because we still loved and missed each other. Eventually Kim found another boyfriend also Bi sexual! and we stayed good friends.

So I was now officially on the "Gay Scene" but it wasn't so easy coming out.

Andy was very possessive over me. He was a bit of a hard nut, a gangster type and very sexy. I was with him on and off for about 2 years. I used to work the lunchtime session at the Talbot then get the train down to Brighton most days. I'd go to Andy's we would then go to the Curtain club because he had to work and then we would go back home. In the morning I would catch the train back to Cuckfield if I wasn't too hung over. He watched me all the time. I was ok talking to his mates or some of the younger lads like me, but wow betide any of the older men not in the clique. If they so much as looked at me, he'd just go up and throw them against the wall or throw them across the dance floor. I hated it. He was never ever violent towards me. He used to apologise and say he just saw red if anyone looked at me. He said "I know these guys they're like me and there after you and want you in their bed. They all like the chickens" Chickens are what we were called then if you were under 21. Now the word is Twink. Andy's wrath was often fuelled by too much brandy.

He'd start off on light ales then people would bring him brandies over to the door and he'd get through a lot!

Other than that we were very happy. Sober he was a very nice man with a great sense of humour. I know now that he wasn't faithful to me; I would have gone mad if I knew. He was a bastard in some ways. In others very kind and sweet. He gave me some very nice jewellery, was generous when we were out etc and very loving.

Some people including my mother when she found out thought he had taken advantage of me and wanted to murder him. Terrie Varley called him a dirty Coont and to stay away from him. But I knew my own mind, I was no pushover ever. If I hadn't have wanted to go with him I would not have. It could have been worse. Instead he tried to guide me in the right direction. When I started making lots of gay friends nearer my own age, he would go mad if I started camping it up a bit with the others for fun.

"Don't be like all the others acting like a load of silly queens, your different to them" Still for a while in the future I did go through a camp phase to fit in I suppose.

I wasn't thinking about another job, I was happy working for mum and dad, I was good behind the bar and popular with all the ladies who lunched I got bought lots of drinks and had lots of laughs.

I was happy with Andy and my secret night time life in Brighton. I did the odd bar shift in the Curtain Club and over the road in the other gay club called The Palace pier club. Again the owner fancied me, knew I was underage but gave me my own bar to run, there were two. The first night somebody hit someone over the head with a soda siphon and I had my finger permanently on the panic button petrified.

To get a late licence in those days they had to be called supper clubs. The clubs would serve a light meal and the customers had to eat it. In The curtain club it was always spam, packet mashed potatoes and baked beans, served by fat Debbie (Roger) through a serving hatch onto a paper plate. At the Palace Pier club it was a salad. Same food every night all year. Occasionally Mike and Wendy (Peter) would go mad and let Debbie serve a tinned curry and rice, but not often.

(It was common on the gay scene for gay men to be given a women's nickname) This was just for fun. People would say if he was a women he'd be called Doris or Sharon etc. It was known as your camp name. It's died out now, but it was harmless and just for laughs, I never did have one thank God.)

Andy knew everyone and some guys in London were starting the first gay travel agents called Man Around. They were setting up a holiday complex in Mykonos in Greece for gay men only.

They asked Andy if he would go and be their holiday Rep there. After a lot of humming and haring he said yes. I was really upset at this obviously as I did not want him to go.

There were lots of tears and arguments. Andy promised to send for me as soon as he could and I could go out and join him there, he would find us an apartment and then get me sent over. Man Around agreed to this. To be fair to Andy he did try often to get me to go over. Something always happened and it was cancelled at the last minute. I suppose I was on standby and if they managed to sell the holiday at the last minute I lost out. Neither of us had money for flights and travel. It was a difficult place to get to then with no direct flights.

He wrote me a few lovely letters, not many.

He was having the time of his life. I got in with quite a racy trendy crowd and still went clubbing most nights.

Now if I needed somewhere to stay in Brighton. I stayed at the house Andy rented for a while but one of the lodgers got fed up with me parking myself on them, quite rightly, although I think Andy was still paying the rent. Paul had moved into a large flat in Brunswick terrace with his boyfriend Chris and offered me a room. Chris was away a lot with work so we had the place to ourselves... party central.

I told mum and dad I was moving out. Things had got difficult at home. I told them both one night I was gay. My mother's reaction was anger she said "Go to Bed I didn't raise a Queer!" This surprised me because mum and I were always incredibly close. My dad put his arms around me told me he loved me and that it didn't matter. I had expected the reactions to be the other way around.

The atmosphere was strained with my mother and me. I just wanted to go. Now looking back I was still 16 not quite 17 very young. I'd been having an affair with a 42 year old man. She must have been worried sick.

So I moved to Hove and had what I call my gap year. We didn't have them then. You left school, got a job or if you were very clever went to University. We didn't have backpacking holidays and rack up student debts like the kids do today.

So with Andy far away, a new man entered the scene (a combination of the fickleness of youth and raging hormones). I signed on the dole like it seemed everyone else had in Brighton. I got £9.00 a week. My rent was £8.00 pw Chris wouldn't let me claim housing benefit but he used to let me off paying the rent a lot. Chris Price was a lovely decent man.

I'd flirt with other men but hadn't been unfaithful to Andy ever. Then I met this guy called David Simons. He was different to Andy a film buff who was the camera man at the Brighton film theatre. They showed all the avant guarde films of the time. He saw me and made a beeline for me. He had a hypnotic quality and was quite Svengali like looking back. Terrie Varley warned me against him saying he'll hurt you! He has all the others. But who listens? And he would spend most nights with me in Hove. While keeping his much nicer apartment around the corner for his other love interests unbeknown to me of course. It was a very promiscuous era. The tail end of the swinging 60's and pre AIDS. But I was old fashioned like that and didn't sleep around.

He was a horrible man sometimes. Deeply mixed up about his childhood. He was cruel. He could twist things he'd done to make it look like it was your fault and you would end up believing him. He was a serial philanderer and spun all of us a load of lies. He was a good lover and very romantic at times but it wasn't a nice relationship.

Once when I caught him chatting this lad up, he said 'there's nothing in it I promise, I've just offered him a lift home as he's missed his last train. Come with us if you don't believe me.' So I went, big mistake. David was drunk and crashed the car near devils dyke a country area on the outskirts of Brighton. The car went up in the air rolled and landed upside down. Eventually I managed to crawl through the back window of the car. We were ok we thought. Because he didn't want to get caught drink driving he said you're ok love you can walk home (the nerve) it was about 3 miles. Luckily the car didn't blow up. It wasn't his it belonged to a sugar daddy he had I knew nothing about and wasn't insured either.

I can't remember what happened to the other guy. It was all a daze. I remember the next day still in shock. I did start getting headaches and back ache. The back ache plagues me even today. I went home to Cuckfield for a few days told mum and dad (partly) what had happened. They were mortified but I wouldn't let them do anything about it.

Unbelievably I went on seeing him. He had such a hold over me.

Years later I bumped into him in the Queens Arms in George Street. He'd been living in Germany where his mother was from. He asked me out to dinner and I said no. I was quite offish with him. Later that night he drove to Beachy Head near Eastbourne and drove himself over the top and committed suicide. Apparently he had found out he had contracted Aids. What a sad ending.

42 club cast including Barry Smith
and Syd lewis bottom right

42 club pantomime programme.

Andy pier

Andy and me curtian club

Angie and me after the Afro club
aged 16

David Simons curtain club

Early terrie varley

Me and nap

Me Terrie v, Ken tate,
John and Clarrisa

Nap as an A sexual of the future
curtain club

Mum and terrie varley my 21st

21

I'm In with the In crowd

My friends at this time were the fashionable Brighton set. Led by two welsh guys known as Nap and Marsha. Both from Cardiff they were great fun, very naughty and outrageous. Naps real name was Geyhard Naperallia and Marsha was Martin. Nap was very well educated and from a good family, but they threw him out and disowned him when they found out he was gay. He had also been to drama school.

Nap was incredibly tall, very slim and very camp but not the prettiest. Marsha was what we called a clone. Denim jeans checked shirt and a moustache, but he was also very camp and very attractive. They made an unlikely duo. There was David the dancer, Black pearl (a beautiful looking little black guy Marsha's boyfriend for a while) Keith (kitty) who had a very good looking wealthy boyfriend called Ricky (who I had a mad crush on and vice versa) Two transgender male to females also from Wales called Steph and Mandy, a girl known to all as Annbag, a lovely guy called Giam, Paul and me. Another friend was my David's ex a sexy boy called Paul (Angel) and his outrageous pal called Tony.

Tony Goldie.

Tony (Goldie) ran a hairdressing salon in a rough part of Brighton, We used to sit upstairs above the shop and watch and listen to him through the holes in the floor insulting the customers. "look at your 'air' dear I bet you've been up all night again doing punters and sucking cock, look at it, it's dreadful" These old girls loved it and would cackle with laughter. He was from a travelling family and swore he was born underneath a dodgem ride in the East end of London. He knew a tasty recipe for Odgie pie. (Hedgehog) I never tried it.

Years later I became good friends with him again, He had moved to Benidorm in Spain and was doing the same thing again now under the name of Goldie, a bit of a legend in Benidorm. He now runs a hotel in Blackpool called "Goldies". One day he arrived on the beach in Benidorm long, black hair in a pony tail and sat on the end of my sun bed. He was on his mobile to his friend Jimmy, who was having a wild affair with this Arab guy. In broad cockney and at the top of his voice he started to give Jimmy some advice.

"I'm telling you gel Ee's a wrong un. I went round to your latte (apartment) yesterday Dolly, not only did he try to ave is wicked way wiv me Dolly EE came out of your bathroom stinking like a fucking perfumeria!" You need to watch yer 'andbag' Dolly!

Well everyone around us just collapsed into laughter. He didn't mean to be funny but his timing was brilliant. His concession to Spanish mentioning the Perfumeria was pure Goldie and he called everybody Dolly.

A Lovely man with a heart of Gold. He is loved by many.

Punk was just starting and Steph and Mandy embraced it very early as did Annbag. They were very cool and hung out with Boy George and Marilyn in London. I was the youngest in the group and they all mothered me. Steph and Mandy both paid for their transitions from male to female by "going on the game" they didn't really have a choice, there was no funding available or much help then. They used to service punters in shop doorways or at the back of pubs. Always straight men too. After they had had a drink they couldn't tell the difference. If they could they tried to get away with just giving blow jobs saying they had their period. Mandy got hers done first and dragged me into the ladies with her to show me her new "Nunu" proud as punch she was. I said shame you can't cum anymore, "oh I can love, over and over again" she said estatically.

Punk didn't appeal to me I was to square. I didn't like the music either. I had long shoulder length hair that I used to blow dry right back and use curling tongs. So I looked like the actress Farah Fawcett with a moustache. I wore high waisted flared trousers with 3 belts and wedge heeled shoes. It was fun watching those that did like the punk style make all their weird and wonderful creations out of bin liners and safety pins. We were an unlikely bunch of friends but it worked and we had some great times.

Paul eventually moved out of Brunswick Terrace and Nap and Marsha moved in. Nap took Paul's place and slept with Chris... to cover the rent..... And Marsha shared a bedroom with me. Or on the couch if David stayed over. They all quite liked him because he was intelligent and sophisticated and knew a lot about films and music but thought he treated me like shit.

Oh the fun we had then. We never had any money or hardly any food. It was a lesson in survival. Our priority was going out at night to have a good time. We would share clothes, money and food.

The spam mash n beans at the curtain club became our main meal of the day. If we had food I'd make a huge saucepan full of soup with anything that I could find, on hot days we would picnic on the beach opposite huge saucepan and all.

When we were really hungry Nap would go out and shop lift. He often dressed up as Old Mother Riley. The full regalia. Long black skirt, white blouse, black shawl, head piece the lot. He was hilarious. He would go into full character. Yelling "where's me daughter" (the characters catch phrase) as he cycled around town with a dead stuffed budgie strapped to the handlebars of his bike.

He used to love coming down St James Street in Brighton from the top at great speed downhill in full Riley drag with his legs sticking out wide screeching "Where's me Daughter" people stopped open mouthed and then burst into laughter, it cheered everyone up. Brighton was full of eccentric characters then and a lot of fun.

This old M. R drag gave him a good disguise if he decided to hit the food shops. "Marsha I must feed the children, they cannot and will not starve, not as long as I'm their Mother!" and off he'd go to find food. Trouble was he was as blind as a bat and far too vain to wear glasses. So he'd sweep into a shop in full drag or something outrageous with a type of opera cloak on over the shawl with lots of pockets in, start with the "Where's me daughter" routine and fill his pockets with whatever came to hand while the staff were to over-come with shock to notice him pilfering.

One day he had gone into a health food store by mistake think-ing it was a grocer's and came back with loads of tinned lentil burg-ers. They were disgusting and bounced off the floor if you dropped one. Still he had got a lot so we ate those for about two weeks.

At night we would start at the Heart and hand pub, buy half a lager each if we could afford it. If not they told me to head for the toilet and go out one at a time and take it in turns to nick a drink off a table. You'd walk around with it until someone offered to buy you a drink then get a clean glass. Then you'd say oh do you know my friends this is so and so and we are all drinking Pils lagers. This would be me or one of the younger pretty ones. A bit Oliver Twist when I think about it and I'm ashamed of it now, but we were young and stupid but never stupid enough to take drugs. At least I wasn't.

Nap and Marsha would occasionally do a bit of pick pocketing too. I never did. They had both lived hand to mouth in Cardiff and still did. So they were survivors but it was not my style at all.

My mother also helped out in this "gap year" I'd go home now and again to the Talbot and she would let me fill a big blue laundry bag full of food from the pubs freezers, so we all ate well now and again.

Even though Andy was in Greece and I hadn't heard from him in months, he got to hear about the crowd I was mixing with and the fact I had taken up with David. A friend of his warned me "be careful Jeremy he is having you followed" I got a phone call one night at the curtain club from him in Greece. He started ranting and raving at me. "What the hell are you hanging around with that bunch of Queens for? They are no good? And I've heard all about that Cxxt David Simons. I shall kill him when I come" back etc etc.

I said you were the one who left; you are supposed to have sent for me. Eventually he did but I never got there. Always cancelled.

So I carried on with David for a bit longer, when I couldn't stand it anymore it finished. I met another guy who was huge and a pub doorman in a tough pub in London who liked me a lot. He went and told David to leave me alone and he did. Like most bullies he was a coward.

It's hard to describe to people what that relationship was like as I'm quite a tough person myself now. It wasn't physically abusive but it was mentally.

Marsha had got a job in an antique shop run by the outrageous Maria. She was an ex bunny girl who was Victor Lownes (the owner of the playboy clubs) girlfriend for a while. She married well and opened this shop in the lanes in Brighton. I would hang out there some days, we would sit in the window (with floor to ceiling glass, the shop front was raised so you had to go up steps to get into the shop) and play cards or backgammon. Maria's party piece was to wait for some school boys to go past and then she'd open her legs and flash them, she never wore knickers. We used to wet ourselves laughing at the reaction.

I've made her sound like a tart but she wasn't. She was very well spoken (with a light Welsh burr) sophisticated, beautifully dressed and uber cool and if she didn't like you, a hard bitch. She had two pet ducks she used to take for walks around the lanes with long gold chain on them. Often she would get bored and say come on boys lets go for a drink and we would close the shop, jump into her convertible and whiz around town, ending up in an afternoon club, usually the 42 club or the Curtain club which was also opened in the afternoons, but there were dozens of these tucked away in Brighton. Maria was loaded and loved our company and was very generous. I was often the beard for her and this gorgeous blonde guy, he said he was straight, and he worked at the curtain club. She was having an affair with him. So was I. (after David)

One of the drinking clubs was the Regency club ran by the legendary 'Baby Jane' (Ronnie with a dreadful toupee,) who sat on the door. A great big fat guy, he never smiled. One day I remarked on this and someone said he can't smile his mouth is full of 50ps, which was the entrance fee. That was his fiddle. Every now and then he'd get up and go and spit them into his coat pocket.

It was a great time and part of growing up. There was a party somewhere every night, but after a year of living this wayward lifestyle and being in that miserable relationship my weight had plummeted to about 8 stone.

My mother and her aunt my lovely aunt Nel came down to visit and I went to meet them in Brighton. We were walking down Western Road when my aunt said to me, "Jeremy are you alright? You're not yourself, you've lost your spark" She was right I was suffering unknowingly from depression, one of many bouts' I would battle throughout my life. I was also suffering from exhaustion and malnutrition. A few minutes later I collapsed, just fainted. It was only quick. I managed to get up. My mother said. Right that's it you're coming home and your staying home. I didn't put up much of a fight.

22

RETURN TO THE TALBOT

So after a few days rest and recuperation and lots to eat. I started work with my parents.

This was more than my old job and I worked 5-6 days a week doing various bar shifts lunchtime and evenings and helping in the kitchen when needed and waiting on tables.

I was a good barman. I've always been a chatterbox so mixing with the older customers wasn't hard. I had a group of "ladies who lunch" as regulars. They would sit at the bar everyday knocking back the gin and tonics and white wine telling me all their problems with their husbands, who could get it up, who couldn't etc. I learnt about vaginal warts, prolapses things most 17 year olds didn't need to or know about.

I would make them howl with laughter at my stories. They would buy me loads of drinks (brandy and coke at that time) I'd sleep it off in the afternoon break and do it all again at night.

It wasn't just laughs, I worked hard to. I started to learn the business properly, all aspects of it from cellar management, how to serve a drink properly. Portion control in the kitchen, profit and loss, bookwork, restaurant management and customer relations.

I learnt far more from working with my parents than I did then if I'd had stayed at the Old Ship Hotel and done day release at Brighton tech.

I always worked well with my parents even then, I was still a teenager so could be a bit naughty about getting up and getting back on time but overall it was a happy period.

I still saw London friends but not so often and whenever I could I would slip off to Brighton and the 42 club and the Curtain and Palace pier clubs.

On my 18th birthday my Mum said oh 18 is not important, 21 is the big birthday so I assumed she meant it. So on my 18th I went to Brighton. My mum said don't be late getting back, you have to work tonight. I went off to see Terrie V at the 42 club I would help her clear up when she closed at 6pm and we would go off to the spotted dog gay pub. This was often our routine in those days.

The spotted dog in Middle Street was run by Ray Bishop and his partner Derek known to all as Della. Ray had a nasty habit. Anyone entering the pub wearing a tie, he would cut it off and pin it to the ceiling, there were lots of them! He was a bit strange; however Della was a darling, very kind and very camp. They had thrown a surprise party for my 18th with all my Brighton friends. It was marvellous. Nap had knitted me a scarf; it was so long it went from the street entrance through the two bars and out of the back door.

I was having a ball when the phone went and it was my mother saying where are you? I told her about the surprise party, she said well you'll have to hurry up there are people here to see you to.

So I got the train back and a cab to the pub, which was full of customers that I liked, and Cuckfield friends and old family friends. Mum and Dad had arranged a surprise party there too. With a buffet and champagne the full works. I was inundated with gifts from the customers so many very well thought out and personal it touched me. (It was the same on my 21st although a bigger affair)

It ended up as our parties always did with me on the piano and the whole pub singing their hearts out. Great fun and legal at last.

One rainy day sitting at the bar in the 42 club Terrie decided to book a holiday, she had lots of brochures. She said "that'll do! A week in Lloret de mar Spain anybody want to come?" I said yes please I've never been abroad. She said "good its fooking cheap luv I'll have to book it quick." So we went with her daughter Clarrissa aged 15 going on 30 at the time Marsha came and a nice guy called Ken Tate. (Ken went on to own the famous Prompt corner restaurant in Brighton with partner Alan.) Last was Pixie Paul a nice guy my age who's party piece when drunk was threading a red ribbon through the holes in his foreskin! (He'd been butchered as a baby during circumcision) It was my first time flying and overseas. Unless you count the Isle of white.

We all had a great time and these holidays that Terrie arranged were to be known forever more as Varley Tours. She never minded who went as long as they paid up their instalments on time. She was kind this way and would take people who were on their own and wouldn't have gone on holiday otherwise. She might call them all the coonts under the sun after they got back but she always did it. I went on two of these, the second time to Tenerife, with Della and a guy called laughing John. Another hilarious week. Terrie was very excited because we were going on Freddie Lakers Skytrain. "It'll be like going on the fooking Concorde darlin but bigger!"

Another very famous pub landlady who took her customers on holiday was Winnie Sexton, who owned the Cricketers around the corner from the 42 club and near the lanes. This was another regular stop off for us. The Cricketers was full of gays, theatricals and other characters. Winnie ran it on her own, she never married. She had a wonderful gin soaked voice, always dressed in Christian Dior or similar and smoked through a long cigarette holder. She was a devout catholic who used to take anybody who was one of her regulars who was sick to Lourdes for a cure. She would do this once or twice every year and pay for it.

She also use to throw the after show party on opening night for any shows on at the Theatre Royal so it was always full of actors.

A lovely woman she would do something very nice for me too in years to come.

Andy eventually came back from Mykonos, he had to leave as some of the locals didn't take kindly with the attention he paid to some of their sons. We carried on together in a fashion for a while but it had run its course. We drifted apart eventually but always remained friends. I only have fond memories of him now.

Around this time I got friendly with two guys from London. Tony and John. I met Tony on a day off at the bar at the 42 club, he was at the bar with a friend, and they had a day off from London and had come down for the races. Tony ran the Eleusis a straight club in Fulham south west London.

He was very smartly dressed good company and generous at the bar to everybody. We got on very well and he said he had a long standing boyfriend called John, I was surprised as Tony didn't come over as gay at all. I told him my parents owned a pub and where it was. To my amazement he turned up with his pal as we opened the next morning at 10.30 am! He did this for several days drinking vodka and orange juice. He drank my Dad out of orange juice in two days and we always kept a full stock.

In the afternoons he'd drive me (I know we didn't think much about it in those days) In his very smart car down to the 42 club and then back again to work in the evenings, (my capacity for alcohol was huge in those days) My parents liked him to. There was nothing romantic or sexual going on we just hit it off as friends. At the weekend he came down from London with his boyfriend John Braine who has remained my dear friend to this day and became a very big part of my life. We all got on famously.

John and Tony became regulars at The Talbot driving down from Wandsworth most weekends for a while. I was able to introduce them to some of the Cuckfield crowd.

By then I had become firm friends with the Harris Family from Balcombe nearby. Murray Harris was the nephew of the legendary Bomber Harris the hero from World war two who had masterminded the bombing of Dresden in Germany. Murray was the editor of motor magazine and was married to the divine

Althea and they had three lovely daughters. Gabriel, Juliette and Chantelle.

Juliette and I were the same age. The whole family were quite eccentric and bohemian. They lived in a very large Jacobean house, tucked away in the countryside. It was what was called a safe house. They were given it after the war for protection because of Bomber Harris's high profile.

I spent a lot of happy days there around that time. memories of playing badminton and croquet in the grounds, sipping Pimm's loaded with gin, Listening to Edith Piaf classics on an old wind up gramophone on the terrace it was all very Brideshead revisited, (on a small scale) Murray and Althea would come down to the pub most evenings and lunchtime at weekends and invite me back for the afternoon or evening after my shift.

There were always lots of people there. Boys from Worth abbey school, family, Murray's sister Sandy had been in the French resistance and was a world champion backgammon player, I liked her a lot. Also around the house often was a very pretty girl who went to drama school and eventually became a big Hollywood film star Greta Scacchi.

I was able to introduce Tony and John to this family and it was quite different from the kind of life that they led in those days and they got on very well with Murray and Althea. I very rarely stayed at night because if it was cold the ice would form on the inside of the windows. Murray like most country house owners was very conscious of the heating bills.

If it was a night party I'd get a lift up with two of our regular customers Brian Paradise and his girlfriend Michelle who lived opposite the Talbot. Brian was very good looking, he looked like David Wilke a famous swimmer at the time. I had a huge crush on him, he used to flirt like mad and we did have a brief affair. He died very young I'm sorry to say.

By now I was openly gay and the word soon got around.

The boys who had bullied me at school and their older brothers started using the Talbot, with my parents keeping a strict eye on them. I'd become friendly with them, when Paul who also left Brighton too, had got a job as barman in the Burrell arms in Haywards Heath where the local "lads" hung out. After some teasing and banter on both sides we all got on quite well.

I became quite close to a few of them. I'm not exaggerating when I say, that 90% of them made a pass at me if we were alone. This was quite a turn around and I was quite shocked but only one of them had the pleasure.

23

CHANGING DIRECTION

My social life now started to revolve around Cuckfield and London. Brighton was going through a strange phase. There was a new licensing officer a real swine. A born again Christian, he hated gays and did not approve of Brighton's club culture. He started to go after the clubs, raiding them for after hours drinking, letting non members in, anything he could get on them to close them down.

This was also the era for resurgence in what became known as the "pretty Police" A good looking police man would pick up a gay man for sex in public toilets and sometimes after receiving a blow job they would arrest the victim outside for gross indecency. This caused real fear and there were many suicides throughout the country.

Brighton was no exception. This atmosphere caused clubs to shut down, gay bars turned into straight bars and there was a general feeling of fear in the air. Many of the Brighton gay community started to leave and moved to Bournemouth or like most of my friends to London.

I still went down on my day off occasionally to see Terrie V, or I would go and stay with John and Tony in London.

I was always welcomed at John and Tony's flat in Wandsworth. John took me to my first Gay pub in London 'The Union Tavern in Camberwell'. A huge drag cabaret pub in south London. We saw the famous Marc Flemming. Then we started using the Vauxhall

Tavern where there was drag every night. In those days it was two bars. One side full of drunk Irishmen and the locals, the other full of Gay people. It worked! Lee Paris was the master of ceremonies and used to do a drag show or introduce other acts who performed on the horse shoe shaped bar while he sat in a huge swing seat attached to the ceiling. If we were brave we would pop over to the 'Elly' The elephant and castle. It had a reputation despite being a gay pub for punch ups. The landlord used to cash the giros (unemployment cheques) for the down and outs who lived in Rowtown house along the road.

Sometimes we would venture over to Earls Court to the Colherne, A famous leather bar where allsorts went on. We stood out like sore thumbs dressed to the nines with as much jewellery and gold chains we could get away with. It was the fashion. Then we would end up at the Copacabana club and disco, a really smart gay club that was intimate and friendly. Freddie Mercury and Kenny Everett were regulars.

We would also pop up to the west end and go to the AnB Club and The Regency Club in Soho owned by a friend of mine I'd met at the 42 club Colin (Spud) Murphy. Or the massive nightclub Heaven occasionally.

24

"A Gangsters Moll"

I first met Spud (Colin Murphy) when he came down to Brighton for the horse racing.

He would end up at the 42 club with his entourage. Spud was terribly obese at least 25 stone. He was gay had a lovely bi boyfriend called MG. He owned several clubs in London and a famous restaurant in Kensington called 'The Cafe Fleur'. He had a chauffeur, a Rolls Royce and a Bentley. He was also despite his reputation as a villain a kind and thoughtful gentleman.

He took a shine to me and invited me up to his club, (the Regency) in Soho if ever I was up that way. So I went with Cuckfield Paul and eventually John Braine. The Regency was a bit on the seedy side, and had its share of rent boys as customers. It was a bit like the 42 club in Brighton a mixture of gays, gangsters, publicans and theatricals, (except no rent boys at the 42, Madam would not have allowed that!)

Spud obviously had a thing for me. His boyfriend Mg had decided to go straight again and met a lovely girl and had a baby and lived near me in Burgess Hill Sussex so there was a vacancy.

I wasn't interested at all. He liked me he said because I was different, "classy", which was nice but I still wasn't interested. One night I left it too late to go back to Cuckfield and he invited me to stay the night. I was very wary. "No it's alright babe, I won't lay a hand on you just stay with me the night for company" I did and that's all it was. He was quite lonely I suppose. That's the truth!

He liked his food and I was delighted when he took me for a champagne breakfast at the Cavendish hotel in Mayfair at 4am. The Cavendish had been featured in a popular television series called the 'Duchess of Duke Street' and I was a big fan. Rosa Lewis the owner of the Cavendish (known as the Bentinck in the programme) was a famous cook and the mistress to King Edward the 7th and had made the hotel notorious.

After breakfast, I expected to go to some mansion while I sat in the back of the chauffeured Rolls Royce. We ended up in this tatty block of flats in Hounslow, miles out from the west end. He said "I had to move out here babe because I kept getting robbed in me house in Regents Park. Even here the fuckers try to rob me." Pointing to the ceiling he showed me a big square that had been cut out of the ceiling and re plastered. "The bastards got on the roof of the flats and sawed right through to get to me safe. Lowered themselves in so as not to trip the alarm off the bastards." I was amazed.

In the morning he said "I'm sorry babe I was going to send you home in one of me cars but the Bentleys in the garage and I need the Roller for a bit of business later, do you mind getting a cab." I said no I don't mind where's the nearest tube? "No I'm not sending you on a tube here's a oner get a cab home to Cuckfield."

Well I was shocked, a hundred pounds was a hell of a lot of money in the 1970's. When I got in the taxi the cab driver said where do you want to go? I said take me to the nearest tube station. I got the train from Victoria back to Haywards Heath station.

When I got off I walked straight over to the taxi rank got in and said take me to the shops. I was dying to go and spend some money. When we got up to the shops they were all closed, it was half day closing.

I used the Regency and AnB club regularly for a while. I met a guy up there called Michael Oxford. He managed a pub called The

Prince of Wales in Drury Lane. He was the ex partner of Danny La Rue. I dated him for a while but he wasn't my type so it didn't develop into much.

But one night he said come up to town, Spuds having his birthday party at the Cafe Fleur in Kensington. I arrived in my casual jeans and a blouson baggy top as I had made a day of it and gone shopping up the west end with my sister Deborah.

I was mortified when I arrived, as it was a sit down black tie formal dinner for about 100 people. It turned out that Michael hadn't been invited to the dinner and neither had I.

Spud spotted me and waved to me to come over and had a waiter put a chair next to him at the top table for me. As I walked through the restaurant in my jeans, with a carry a bag under my arm with clean pants and socks for the morning, everyone was staring at me wondering who I was. I was so self conscious I tripped over the handbag of this very elegant Spanish looking woman looking like Maria Callas, dressed to the nines covered in gold and diamonds. As I tripped my clean pants flew out of the bag and landed in her soup! She just laughed said don't worry about it, go and sit down. Eileen White was very kind to me that night. She would play a big part in my life, many years later.

Spud made a big fuss of me, said sorry I never asked you I didn't think you'd like being with all these old fogies what are you doing with that pratt Michael anyway?

I was in my element I ended up dancing on the tables while the elegant Eileen played the spoons. I had a lovely meal, Spud had arranged for fresh strawberries to be flown in out of season. The champagne flowed all night and then back to both clubs with lots of the guests for a party that went on until the early hours.

Michael was left in the bar with another old friend Brian Skinner who also had not been invited.

Not many years later Spud decided that London as he knew it had had it. Styles change he was from the era of the Krays and Richardson's they were all now in Prison. His club was dated and he moved up to Blackpool and opened a casino. Unfortunately the local Gangsters didn't take kindly to a Cockney moving in onto their turf. He was murdered, hit around the head with a sawn off shotgun the Sun newspaper said.

He was a lovely man.

25

FALLING IN LOVE AGAIN

My life continued like this for ages. I'd work at the pub, we would have lots of parties, fun nights where we would dress up. Me as Shirley Bassey or some other hero of mine. Cringe making now looking back. We catered for lots of weddings and functions. We had a very successful pub.

My mother became the Mayor of Cuckfield and created the cuckoo fayre which she opened with the famous star Edward Fox. The Fayre runs to this day. Mum raised a lot of money for local charities during her reign. I don't know how she found the time. Always a grafter my mother, even after cooking 70-80 lunches, if one of the elderly regulars was sick she would go round to their house with a tray of hot food after the lunchtime session.

My social life was good. Either in Brighton or going to see a west end show with John Braine or The Vauxhall Tavern in South London.

The year was 1980 I was 19. John and I always made an effort to go and see an act that was becoming very famous at the time known as the Trollettes.

The Vauxhall had undergone a major refit and was now one big bar with a raised tier of seating at the back like an old music hall. There was a large floor space. A big raised stage and a long bar the length of the pub.

One night March the 27th 1980 John and I were sitting in the raised tier watching the act probably the Trollettes (David Raven and Jimmy Court) an outrageous cod drag act which was mostly ad lib, with singing, occasional fire eating, mayhem causing, funny and hysterical, when I ran out of matches. I smoked and smoking was legal inside of a building then. Looking around I caught the eye of this very handsome man with beautiful blue eyes and a short trimmed beard in his 30's 40's and went over and asked for a light.

He blushed bright red, smiled, gave me a light and I went back to sit with John. I said I've just met the man I'm going to live with for the rest of my life. John looked at me as if I'd gone mad and said, come on I'm taking you home you've had too much to drink, I said don't be daft lets go to the Copacabana club in Earls court.

As we were walking to the bar in the Copa I literally bumped shoulders with the man I had met in the pub. Colin Bradshaw bought me a drink and we have been together now for nearly 40 years. Fate or what?

26

MAYBE IT'S BECAUSE I'M A LONDONER

Colin was in the merchant Navy. He worked one week on and one week off for Townsend Thoreson. So we were able to see each other fairly well. He was based at Southampton and I was in Cuckfield. For me it was love at first sight, for Colin it took a week or so longer. Mainly because he was very nervous about my age (19, you still had to be 21 the legal age to be gay) and also the age difference. He was 42.

John and Tony used to put us up which was good of them. However once we had decided to live together we started to look for a flat in London. Colin wanted to move back to London and I was happy to.

We found a lovely little one bedroom flat in Albert Bridge road in Battersea, near the park. It was a smart part of Battersea, which was then being gentrified. The gas works were still open and there was a strong smell of candle wax from Prices the candle factory up the road.

This for me was my first proper home of my own. I loved it. We moved in around July 1980 my 20th birthday. My parents were not happy about the arrangement at all. My mother refused to meet him saying he was far too old. I wasn't into older men particularly it's just how things worked out. The same with Andy, but I did like men a bit older than me then, men my own age seemed infantile to me.

This caused difficulties for the first year. It was quite a wrench for me again. I had settled down in Cuckfield working at the pub, lots of friends, busy social life.

Now here I was in a part of London I didn't know very well with any friends except for John and Tony in nearby Wandsworth.

When Colin was home it was fine, we were busy making our new home our own, we went out every night to the Vauxhall or for dinner. His family, Mother Nel, Brother Bill and Sister Audrey who were dotted about South West London welcomed me with open arms. All through out the years I've stayed friends with his family. Especially sister Audrey and nieces Sian and Connie who are more like cousins to me because we are similar ages.

When he was at sea I was on my own. I went out with John once a week but that was about it.

I rowed a lot with my mother. My sister was in Barnes near Putney not too far away but she was at work all day.

So I grew quite lonely. Colin earned very good money so I didn't have to work but I started looking for a job.

I got a job cheffing in Tutton's restaurant in Covent Garden and hated it. I was the only English person in my section. So that didn't last long, plus the pace was extraordinary 100 meals an hour!

I worked in a few other places around Mayfair, Green Park, but couldn't settle. Eventually I got quite ill again with my nerves and my weight plummeted to about 8 stone. The stress of leaving home again, a new relationship, jobs, a rift with my mother all contributed to a bit of a meltdown. I was still on tranquillisers from the age of 14. This eventually grew to sleeping tablets as well because Colin snored like the sailor he was. I was always fairly highly strung then and a bit sensitive still.

Eventually things got better. I made some new friends. One called Chipmunk and another called Swales.

Chipmunk (John Moralee) I met one night in the Vauxhall it was very crowded and I accidentally tipped a pint of Guinness over his head. He was shorter than me. I got pushed from behind and whoosh. He was very kind about it and we started chatting. He was very funny, we had the same tastes in music, he didn't give a toss about anything and was very extrovert. He introduced me to Swales Forrest, a good looking blonde, his family owned the largest travelling funfair in London. We are all still friends nearly 40 years later.

So I now started to have a social life while Colin was at sea. The three of us and sometimes John Braine went out most nights of the week. We did the rounds of all the popular gay hangouts of the era. Vauxhall Tavern, The Market Tavern, The Union Tavern at Camberwell, The west end, everywhere there was something going on. Colin joined in when he was home as well. We had many parties at our flat, we always kept a well stocked bar as Colin used to bring home duty free's plus his naval allowance. Half a bottle of Brandy was 50p! It was fun.

I eventually set up a private catering business from home called "Puddings" This was moderately successful. I got a few commissions for corporate functions providing lunches and buffets around Victoria from some of my Cuckfield contacts.

I also got work back in Sussex. Eventually I started doing a few weddings on riverboats on the Thames and these were very good earners.

Christmas approached and my mother wanted me to come home. I'd only agree if Colin could come to. That was not going to happen. So I said right I'll stay in London then. Colin was home Christmas day but had to rejoin the ship Boxing day so we had our first Christmas at home alone and my first and only one since without being with my family. This did not go down well at home. But I needed to put my foot down. I was as strong willed as my mother so we were bound to clash a bit.

I'm glad to say that after that things improved and Colin was welcomed into my family like a son in law and my parents grew to think the world of him.

27

COLIN

Colin is one of the kindest, sweetest, passionate, animal loving people you could wish to meet. He would do anything to help anyone and would open a window for a fly to go out rather than kill it. He's also very shy. His faults are a very short fuse and a terrible temper plus a tendency to be glass half empty while I'm always glass half full. So he's a bit of a contradiction.

Born in Fulham London August 19th 1938 He was a war baby. His Father Cornelius (Con) was a skilled carpenter and worked at the Redifusion Radio and eventually television factory. His mother Helen (Nellie) was a Fulham Girl. She brought up her mother's younger children (her mother had committed suicide due to an abusive husband) as well as her own three children Bill, Audrey and Colin + a little girl who died called Twinkle.) She also worked at the Sunlight laundry for extra money. A tough generation she lived until she was 93 and I was very close to her.

Colin was always a shy child and not academic like his elder siblings, however he had a musical ear (he played the cornet) and was excellent at metal work at school much to his father's disappointment who wanted him to become a master carpenter like himself. Colin Says he was useless at woodwork.

Aged 15 and a member of the air cadets, with a lot of arguing and tears he talked his parents into signing the forms to let him join the RAF (Air force) as an apprentice. He had wanderlust and wanted to see the world. So he left home and progressed through the ranks and became a fully qualified engineer and served 2-3 years in Cyprus on active service.

After a successful career in the Air force he had had enough after several years and bought himself out.

He had various jobs enjoying his freedom. He had lots of girlfriends and the occasional boyfriend.

Completely straight acting nobody guessed he was bisexual.

For a period in the 1960's he got involved with the wrong sorts and was part of a South London gang known by the nickname of "The quality street gang" Sharp dressers in their "Mod" suits and flash cars. Colin's physical strength (short but solid) and driving skills came in handy.

Deciding that the lifestyle perhaps wasn't for him after all, he got various mechanical jobs before joining the merchant navy. Now he indulged his wanderlust and travelled the world on cargo ships and banana boats. A typical sailor with girls in every port. He drank his share of Rum and spent his wages when ashore. He didn't save for rainy days he just lived from job to job.

Colin 1981

Colin and me on my 40th Selfridge
Hotel London July 2000.

Colin and I in moraira winter sun

Colin and me spain 1980

Colin arundel castle

In New York 1988 aged 28   Senior Mechanic

Jeremy

Lovely pic of colin | With Colin July 6th 2019 my birthday.

Me and colin on lollys yacht

28

BATTERSEA BOY

When I met him in 1980 he had just finished a 7 year relationship with a woman. He'd had two long relationships with men before her too. He was reluctant to get involved again so soon but sometimes it just happens.

I was terribly possessive in those days and jealous of anyone from the past. Insecure as hell.

He had been senior mechanic on the QE2 but got another job as senior mechanic on the ferries from Portsmouth and Southampton with Townshend Thoreson as the money was much better and you got lots of time off. Every other week off plus 16 weeks paid holiday a year, incredible.

The unions were strong then and a certain John Prescott was the head of the Seaman's Union. They would strike at the drop of a hat. That's why the conditions were so good.

We were not complaining we had a ball going out, we had a new BMW, and life was good. However I didn't realise that Colin wasn't great with money and soon we had a few debts mounting up. Eventually I took over the financial management side of our life and made sure that we were never in debt ever again.

However with money short for a while, it meant Colin had to cross the strike picket line once or twice to be spat at and shouted at and called a scab. The union didn't pay the rent!

Our "love nest" in Battersea was not meant to last. We stayed about 18 months but our lovely landlords wanted to sell the flat to put towards buying a bigger house for themselves. They offered us first refusal at a bargain price of £17,000. Quite a lot in 1981-2 but that flat is probably worth 650k now. I wanted to buy it, get a mortgage but Colin wasn't interested. Also at that time another great apartment close by came on the market for 24k. I went to look at it and it turned out to be owned by Marianne Faithful Mick Jaggers ex. It was a trendy area and on the way up with people like Marianne who couldn't quite afford Chelsea and it was walkable to the Kings Road, where Saturday lunchtimes were spent in the 'Queens head' and the 'Markham arms'. Both gay pubs then, followed by weekend food shopping in Safeway's. I knew even then it was a great investment but Colin wouldn't listen to me.

Colin had had his name down for some time for a GLC (greater London council) flat, higher rented accommodation. They were not local authority council flats. You had to be working and earn a certain amount of money to qualify to get one. (a good idea they should re introduce) However he did and we did get one.

It was a brand new 1 bedroom ground floor flat with 2 gardens, front and back. The rent was £17 a week. Maybe Colin was right, we had security, a low rent and plenty of money to spend in the pub. The only problem was it was in Tooting. I really did not want to move there, but the flat was really nice and places like that were gold dust for Londoners even then.

It was in a weird part of Tooting In between Tooting Junction station near Mitcham to the south and Colliers Wood to the west. I hated it.

The flat though was lovely, everything brand new. Not overlooked. We soon moved in and I had great fun at Peter Jones in Sloane Square picking out fabrics for curtains and sofas etc. I had always been taught buy the best it will last, so I did. I have never ever bought cheap furniture. Colin had some nice pieces in storage so soon it was looking like a very chic flat in Chelsea not a GLC flat in Tooting.

Chipmunk often stayed over with me instead of his mother's in Earlsfield just down the road, while Colin was at Sea. Swales lived in Mitcham just up the road and came around most days when he wasn't traveling with the fair. Another bonus was I had two friends who lived around the corner, Maisie and Rosina.

Maisie I had been introduced to a few years previously by Tony and John. Tony had worked with her at some point. I met her at a very smart Water rats charity dinner with them at the Grovsner house hotel in Park Lane.

She was a character as was her sister Rosina.

Maisie was as hard as nails with a soft centre if she liked you. When she was younger she had been a rent collector for the notorious crook Peter Rachman. The same type of guy we'd had in Primrose Hill. He owned a lot of flats and houses in Paddington which he used to rent out at high rents to the prostitutes who worked the area near the train station. Maisie would go around and collect the rent from the prostitutes and could perform abortions if necessary. Not sure how she acquired the skill but she did.

After a year of doing this she realised she could make more money on her back than collecting the rent so she set herself up as a prostitute to. She was soon able to buy a house in a respectable suburb for her husband and two daughters with cash. She introduced her sister Rosina, a beautiful brunette to the business. She also taught her how to perform abortions too. Rosina had two children to feed and needed the money. I'm not condoning any of this, it's just the facts. This was always discussed in a matter of fact way but it used to make my stomach churn a bit.

However they were great fun. Loyal friends to. Rosina's daughter Stephanie was a part time lesbian who was in and out of borstal a lot. She taught me how to drive. (Colin had bought me and old Renault to learn in). She would come around to the flat while Colin was at sea with a few cans of Special Brew in a bag and say. "Come on Jel get a couple of these dan yer neck for Dutch courage and I'll take you out for a driving lesson"

I did as I was told and was soon driving up to the west end and back, having learned the basics kangarooing around Wimbledon common with my L plate's on. London was a good place to learn because although it was busy you couldn't really get anywhere very fast so you learned the gear and clutch work well.

Colin also taught me to drive properly when he was home. I drove like that for a couple of years, Down to Cuckfield and back and all around London. Then Colin insisted I take a test and get a legal license. I passed on the second attempt having failed the first time from nerves and being too cautious. Still not bad for someone who never had a formal lesson in his life.

One of my friends was too nervous to take his test and had learned the same way as me. So his boyfriend went and took it for him using his name. This friend did it for a few of our mates. One day his sister said to him "Oh Baz will you take mine for me as well" he looked at her in amazement. "What do you expect me to do go up there in full fucking drag you dopey mare" we all fell about laughing.

You could get away with things like that in those days, there wasn't the technology to check you out.

Having settled in the flat I started up "Puddings" again and got work doing buffets for pub change over's the odd thing here and there. John Braine had trained to be a florist years before and did all the flowers for me for my functions. He would go to Covent Garden and buy arms full of flowers and make beautiful arrangements all from our kitchen in Tooting.

However, I was fed up with catering. I got a job in doughty Street in WC1 for a horticultural magazine called the 'Grower' selling advertising space. I shared a lovely big office with this crazy girl called Georgina. It was my first ever 9-5 job and my last.

I would catch the train from Tooting Junction into Holborn central London and walk to my new smart office. Doughty street is rows of Regency houses, very elegant. Charles Dickens used to live there.

This has to go down as one of the most boring jobs I've ever had. Basically I had a list of potential advertisers to ring up, farmers mainly and try to convince them that the only way they would shift more manure was to advertise it for sale in the Grower.

Can you imagine doing that 7 hours a day? For every 50 calls you make you might get a 1/4 of a page advert, it was soul destroying. Gina and I would start off with a pep talk from our irritating sales boss ("let's take a view on that" Tony) with the intention of selling 6 full pages of adds to be deflated by lunchtime and heading for the door.

This was the best bit of the day. I could wander around leather lane market in Holborn, go and have a pint and stop at a little cafe and have a roast of the day for 50p.

There was a restaurant in Leather lane that used to carve big ribs of beef in the window, the smell was mouthwatering I used to stare in salivating. This was not in my budget however, so the Greek greasy spoon on the corner used to have to do.

To ease the boredom some days we used to arrange a phone link. Remember this was pre computers and mobile phones. Chipmunk used to work for Littlewoods catalogue on the switchboard in Wandsworth. We used to ring him and he would link us up to Gina's gay friend Lloyd James at Reed employment in Dartford via the Littlewoods switchboard. So at a prearranged time we would surreptitiously pour a glass of wine and ring in to what we would nowadays call a conference call, unheard of then.

We would all have a good natter and a giggle. Chipmunk and I had never met Lloyd but we knew we would get on. Like me he was a huge fan of Dorothy Squires and I arranged to meet him at a concert she was giving at the new Barbican centre in 1982. We did get on. Lloyd went on to become a hugely successful entrepreneur and we are still good friends today.

Well I lasted 6 months. Then my contract wasn't renewed. They wanted to try a different approach. I didn't care I was bored stiff, but the money was regular and handy, even if the commute in from Tooting Junction was a bit grim.

29

SAM AND 'THE BARON'

While I was thinking about what to do next I decided to get a dog. Colin was dead against it, but I had made my mind up. I was discussing this one day with my friend Alex, The Baron Fitzroy of Arbery. Chipmunk had introduced me to this colourful character who lived in a tiny studio flat in Lavender hill Battersea. Known as the Baron by all. Alex had been a successful male model in the 1960's under the name of Julian. His bijou apartment sported pictures of him in various artistic poses on the walls. An attractive very tall, thick set man he had changed somewhat and was now slightly bloated. He loved a drink, was terribly grand and affected, a true eccentric and very funny.

He had started life with another name entirely on the outskirts of Coventry in a two up two down terraced workman's cottage. He had bought this and the one next door when he was in the money and let them out to his two maiden aunts. Other than this these days his income was made up by working as a night porter in the hotels in the west end and gentleman's clubs in St James's.

It transpired that the title had been purchased at an auction, but no one was more "to the manor born" than Alex.

So his day times were free and we'd visit him occasionally in this match box of an apartment, (you had to walk sideways to get to the loo) where he would hold court and pour the gin.

Once I got up to get some tonic from the fridge, when I opened the door, all that was inside were eggs. I said Alex you haven't got any food in this fridge except for 6 eggs in the top and they look opaque, clear even. He said with a snort "I should fucking think so dear they've been there since 1964!" he didn't do food as such but he did like cake, lots of it.

He was a colourful sight around Clapham and Battersea. He always wore a black red silk lined opera cloak over tight black trousers and shoes that were monogrammed and had big silver buckles. He was a "Georgie" if you are familiar with EE Bensons Mapp and Lucia, a Dandy.

Chipmunk used to say if he saw him when he was out shopping with his mother he'd dive into a doorway and hide.

This particular day I was telling him about my desire to get a dog. He thought it was a terrific idea and he would come with me to choose one. So off to Battersea Dogs home we went. Sam an Australian terrier literally jumped into my arms when I spotted him. Like a big Yorkshire terrier he was the most loveable dog in the world. Big brown eyes that melted your heart. The Baron said getting emotional, "well you'll have to take him home now dear he has chosen you to be his mother".

All the way home on the top deck of the 44 bus The Baron told everyone on the bus while waving his arms around and displaying the opera cloak off to its finest advantage, that he had been there at the birth! That his daughter (me) was brave but had needed several stitches. On and on he went. Some laughed, some gave me curious sympathetic looks, I just wanted the ground to open up and swallow me. Now I think I'm glad he was like that, there are not enough people around like that now.

Sam was one of the best decisions I made. Colin Loved him after an initial rant, he was the most loving and friendly companion. He would put his arms around your neck and speak to you. He was also a street dog and with the sniff of a bitch on heat he was off. Sometimes for days. After a while I didn't worry as he always came home.

One day I was out walking him near Colliers Wood tube station and some Irish labourers stopped me and one said "is that your little dog" yes I said he replied "Bejesus that dog does some fookin mileage". Apparently Sam used to get on the tube at Colliers Wood and ride up and down on the northern line. Loved him.

30

PIANO BARS

The West End in the 1980's was swinging. One particular favourite haunt was The Piano bar in Soho. Hosted by the then still male
Madam Jo Jo. It was a lovely club with a big concert grand piano
with seats all around it like you used to see in the films. It was situated in Rupert Street behind Stallions night club run by the infa-
mous Tina. You could access it from a door in Stallions which was a
cruisy upmarket gay disco in Falconberg court Soho.

Jo Jo was a shy oriental guy, very friendly and sweet. His boyfriend was Paul Burton who was one of the resident pianists, who
is still a friend of mine. The other resident pianist was Michael
Thorpe Jackson.

Both were brilliant pianists. If I was there Jo Jo used to let me
play in the breaks for drinks. Sometimes if someone was ill or on
holiday I would do a whole night.

I could vamp most things and play show songs, standards and
ballads. The singer Helen Shapiro was starring as Nancy in Oliver
at the time at the Albery theatre close by. After the show Helen and
the cast from Oliver would come in for drink and sit around the
Piano. I got quite friendly with Helen. I could never get her to sing
her big hit "walking back to happiness" though. She would in my
ear but never in public. Sick of it I expect poor girl.

My mother was looking for somebody famous to open her big
charity bottle she kept on the bar in the Talbot. (Edward Fox must

have been busy), so I asked Helen if she would do it. "Of course I will love she said". I said it's quite a drive, she said "don't worry me and the boyfriend will make a weekend of it in Brighton."

Thrilled I rang my mother to tell her and she said. Oh she can't! I've just asked the Vicar to do it! I said so! I've got you a big star. Mum said oh well thank her for me she's very kind but I can't put the vicar off now. I was mortified. Luckily Helen thought it was funny.

The lease must have run out because the club moved to number 50, Frith Street next to Ronnie Scott's Jazz club.

Jo jo now the boss had started to dress in full Glamour drag eventually to change gender into a woman. Gorgeous she was. The line up was the same and this became our new must go to place. The only addition was another transgender woman singer called Rital.

Rital was quite famous on the circuit then. She was foreign possibly Greek or Turkish. Ritual wore a huge red wig and was quite a stunner. She would warble out "Never on a Sunday" Not a great singer but could pull it off because of the glamour.

One night she was sitting behind me while I was playing my set when I turned around and was surprised to see her and another woman fondling each other's breasts and kissing behind the curtain. I thought why go to all that trouble having your willy cut off to become a lesbian. I was naive it's not that uncommon.

Eventually Jo Jo went on to open the world famous Madame Jojos at Paul Raymonds revue bar in Soho, Paul Burton is still playing to packed crowds all around the world, Michael Thorpe Jackson Sadly passed away. Helen Shapiro went on to become a legendary singer in the jazz world. I'm not sure what happened to Rital. I hope she is well.

31

THE CRICKETERS (RAY AND VIV)

So from the west end I ended up playing the Piano at the Cricketers in Battersea! Every Monday night, this glamorous blonde in fox furs and her husband started turning up at the "Vauxhall tavern.' The regulars at the Vauxhall used to congregate in the corner near the stage at the pub. Viv and Ray soon became part of the group. Viv stood out because she was very tall, very loud, good looking (she looked a lot like a big Twiggy) and she could down pints of beer like a navy.

Both originally from Putney south London. They ended up as tenants of a smashing pub called the 'Horse and Chains' in Bushey near Stanmore in north London. They were very successful with a big food trade. I became thick with them because of my pub background. They even invited us out to their holiday villa in Spain for a week, which was great fun. They both spoke Spanish and we were guests of honour at a fiesta in Fuengirola where the local bull fighter through up the bull's bits and pieces for me to catch. I was nearly sick and never went to a bullfight again.

They both though loved the 'Vauxhall', they were both camp and relished in the atmosphere, the laughs etc, plus they could see the amount of money the Irish Landlords Pat and Breda Mc'Connon were taking. A fortune in those days.

Pat and Breda were part of a large Irish pub owning community in south London known affectionately as the "Murphia"

Viv and Ray decided that they too would like a pub like the Vauxhall.

So they sold their very successful pub in Bushey for a run-down rough pub in Battersea park road called 'The Cricketers' The Cricketers had used to be a gay pub years before but had become rundown and used as a local by those of the criminal fraternity that lived on the big council estate behind it. Viv and Ray swopped their country garden in Bushey for a back yard in Battersea, where the only thing to brighten the skyline was the occasional telly being thrown out of the window of the 24th floor of the flats behind.

The plus side was it was enormous with a huge stage. They spent a fortune on renovating it. The opening night was a big success with all the faces on the south London gay scene turning up plus a big line up of celebrities, drag acts, comedians and singers. Even Mrs Shilling a famous socialite turned up wearing one of her son David's enormous hats.

I did all the catering single handedly, the full works salmon in aspic, roast joints of beef and ham, salads puddings, and of course a seafood table with all London favourites of jellied eels and whelks.

John Braine did masses of flower displays and Chipmunk and Swales were ensconced behind the bar.

The next lunchtime the local mob turned up and demanded protection money to "look after the pub" Viv told them to fuck off, so they carted her husband Ray off to the gents and beat him up and flushed his head down the toilets. Not a good start. Eventually they got some villains they knew to have a word and it was dropped.

The pub became a big success for a while. I was resident pianist and occasional compare, the others being Guy Saville and Lee Paris. I played the piano Sunday mornings for Pip Morgan who used to do an act as her Majesty the Queen. It was a polite tribute not rude or irreverent. The Trollettes recorded a live album there and all the top acts appeared nightly.

My old friend Douglas Byng even did a gig there. There was a queue around the block for that. He was amazed at the turn out; we were watching out of the window and chatting about old times upstairs above the pub, looking down on the line along Battersea Park Road. Patrick Newley a well known theatre critic and journalist had booked him and he went down a storm, he was in his late 80's by then.

I'm not sure what went wrong but a combination of Viv's personality (she wasn't everybody's cup of tea) she was prone to flashing herself at people when drunk and the sheer expense of running a venue that size meant that after a few years they had lost a lot of money.

Homeless they had to flee to their villa in Spain. They started a catering business working on various film locations on the Costa del Sol often used for westerns. This too was a success until the film contracts dried up.

Desperate, Ray started handling a few stolen goods for some of the villains that had relocated to the Costa del Sol in the 1980's. He was arrested outside a London Tube station in possession of a valuable clock he was going to sell. He got 2 years in Prison.

Viv over in Spain went into meltdown and crashed her car and became a paraplegic and she had a stroke. This however due to brain damage turned her into a nymphomaniac. She had never been interested in sex before, Ray (nicknamed Rachael) and Viv had always been more like brother and sister. So a lot of the young Spanish fishermen were recruited to help with Viv's "problem" They eventually came back to London.

(Footnote)

Many years later they got hold of my phone number and rang to say they were coming down to visit me in Sussex where I was running a successful club. I was pleased but unable to accommodate them as Viv couldn't manage stairs, so I booked them into a local BnB with ground floor accommodation which I paid for. They arrived late and with a few drinks under their belts, but ok. Viv was walking on sticks and had taught herself to speak again, which was quite remarkable. Ray was very proud of her because she had managed to down 3 pints of Bass Carrington's beer before they came to see me.

She had another pint and sat and talked to one of my customers, managing to insult him within minutes.

Unfortunately when they had phoned me, I had explained that that afternoon Colin and I had been invited to a very smart garden party at a wealthy customer of ours house. Oh can we come? They said. I asked my host and he said of course dear boy any friend of yours is a friend of mine......

Big mistake. After Ray had given everyone his rendition of the song "I love my mother in law (even though she's a dirty old whore)" Viv was sick underneath the table. We managed to put her in her wheelchair and push her down to a bedroom to clean her up (everywhere)We let her sleep a bit as she was too ill to move.

Eventually I got a cab and we took them to the BnB. These people also knew me. They took one look at them and said I'm sorry Jeremy they are not coming in here, they may be sick. I said don't worry they will be fine. Viv was already wheeling herself down the corridor chipping the paint off of the skirting boards with her wheelchair en route to the ground floor bedroom. We opened the door, twenty stone Ray said I can't wait to get to bed, promptly collapsed on top of the twin beds, separating them and was sick all over the floor. Obviously we were asked to leave before they called the police.

We got them back to the club, hurled Viv up the stairs and put her to bed, with a lady friend of mine (Eileen) helping her undress and wash herself again.

The next day you'd have thought nothing at all had happened. Except for a "sorry about last night I must have eaten something that didn't agree with me" Ray went out for a walk and found the local pub where he had several bottles of 'White Shield' Worthington's beer as a livener. He came back very jolly! I cooked them lunch. By now they were feeling better and thinking of staying several days! I said oh no you can't I've got family coming down tomorrow. We waved them off and I broke off all ties never seeing them again.

Two weeks later Chipmunk rang me to say that he had bumped into them and that they were on their way down to see me again that afternoon. I was mortified. I sat on the kitchen floor all afternoon with the lights out (it was winter)

Chipmunk's idea of a joke....it worked.

Sadly Ray died several years ago, I was fond of him and Viv but she was a handful. She is still alive and causing chaos somewhere in London.

32

A Womble

Although we had made our flat in Tooting a really comfortable flat, after a year damp started to appear on the bedroom and sitting room walls which were on the outside of the building. This very quickly progressed to big black patches and grew all up the walls. The council were called in but no matter what they tried they couldn't solve the problem. They gave us a dehumidifier to extract the water and told us to wash the walls down with bleach every day. This went on for a year!

I was furious our lovely Peter Jones curtains and sofa covers were getting covered in mould too, and the new carpets.

I wrote letter after letter to everyone I could think of to get us a transfer. The rent book was only in Colin's name so I had to make out I was him. He couldn't do much he was at sea a lot of the time.

Eventually I got us a transfer to a two bedroom flat in Wimbledon. That's what the postal dress said SW19. It was another higher rented GLC flat. I wasn't keen as it was more Colliers wood than Wimbledon and was really Merton abbey and to near Mitcham for my liking. However it was a take it or leave it choice. My name would go on the rent book too so we moved.

The council found out that when our flat in Tooting had been built. Instead of getting rid of rubbish, the builders had shoved empty black bin liners in the wall cavities and plastered over them. So when it rained the bin liners had filled up with water, hence the damp.

We made the flat in Wimbledon into a really nice pad again. It was bigger than Tooting and we had a spare bedroom. This was handy for Colin's Mum Nellie who stayed with us often for up to 6 weeks at a time on our sofa bed. Now she could have her own room when visiting. I got on very well with Colin's mum. She loved a drink and would come to all the pubs with us despite being in a wheelchair.

Getting a bit short on funds Swales and I decided to do car boot sales. We both had lots of stuff to get rid of so we would get up at the crack of dawn on a Sunday and go and set up at Wimbledon football club. We did well at these boot fairs and sold out of stock quickly. We noticed that when people were packing up they threw all their stuff in a tip. I had a look in and there was some really good things thrown away. So I jumped in this big, massive, deep, council skip and passed anything saleable up to Swales. We had enough for another week and sold it all to.

Encouraged by our success we decided to spread our wings and attend other boot fairs across south London on various days. The novelty wore off in February I think when we were standing ankle deep in snow in a pub car park in Mitcham freezing to death. Great job in the summer but horrible in the rain and the cold.

My next brain wave was to start a sandwich delivery service. There were lots of offices in Wimbledon Town centre and I figured we could make ourselves millionaires in no time.

So Swales and I stayed up nearly all night making various sandwiches, some a bit to exotic Swales thought. "Err who's gonna eat Tuna with Egg? Yuk" I said its Wimbledon Swales they will expect something upmarket not spam and pickle. We realised we didn't have anything to store the sandwiches in so the next morning early we nipped down to the local Tesco and "borrowed" a couple of wire shopping baskets, I lined them nicely with red gingham tablecloths filled them with a selection of sandwiches a menu and a price list and off we went.

Well, we were out all day going from office to office, shop to shop. Even though it was a relatively new concept someone had beaten us to it. Swales tried in the box office at the Wimbledon theatre to no avail and on the way out got stopped by the police to ask if he had a trading or hawkers licence. With his fingerless gloves on and bobble hat he looked like he was selling pegs and lucky heather!

Eventually we sold a cheese and pickle on brown and the man put in a regular order.

Exhausted we made our way back to the car and put the 99 other sandwiches in the boot. Swales said 'I don't think I'll be doing that again! I'm frozen, I've nearly got arrested for hawking without a licence and I'm knackered" I said well that mans placed an order for a cheese and pickle on brown Monday to Friday next week. "Well you fucking well get up and make it and take it to him then cause I'm fucking not"

I said I'm starving there's a McDonalds over there do you fancy a big mac? A big mac! He screamed a big fucking mac! There's a 100 fucking sandwiches in the boot eat those. "No thanks I'm sick of fucking sandwiches" We looked at each other and burst into laughter we were in hysterics!

So that was the end of that!

Swales got some good jobs providing fairground stalls for functions in big pubs or halls. Coconut shies, fish on a rod, candy floss hot dogs etc. One day he was doing a big function at Streatham ice rink. There was a massive bar upstairs above the ice. It had a gay club night on Wednesdays. They needed a palm reader so he phoned me. Get yourself up there tonight I'll put you in a tent and you can do palm readings for 50p a go and keep the money. Ok I said so I took a sort of gypsy costume and armed with a bag of "Special Brew lager" and a sandwich, got myself set up in the tent with low lighting and some mystic bits and pieces and a stool and settled down for the night.

I was always good at reading palms or Duckering as the Gypsies called it. The only thing was I was much better at it after a few drinks. Hence the special brews. Anyway I soon had a few customers and

I was off. After about an hour I saw Swales twitching about out-side. I was reading this women's palm and he held up a sign behind her head. "Hurry up you've got a queue right out to the front door. Charge a Pound!"

Afterwards he said "you were too good and taking too long, the trick is to get them in and out as quickly as possible"

I replied a bit slurry I have a natural gift I can't rush it just to take more money!

My next job was at the Dog and Fox in Wimbledon village. Swales and I both got jobs there. He was in the public bar, while I worked in the functions room where we had different things most night. Wednesdays was gay night known as WAGS. So were Sundays. We had divorced separated and singles nights and boxing dinners.

It was hard work but I enjoyed it. I worked behind the bar and as a silver service waiter. The bar on gay nights was so busy there would be 10-12 of us behind the bar and we would leave the lager taps running and just fill up pints and pass them along the line. This was mainly night work 8pm until 3am. So I decided to get a day job as well.

For a temporary measure I took a job as a private cook for an elderly couple in Wimbledon village around the corner from the Dog and Fox called the Gortways.

They were Hungarian and had escaped the revolution by hid-ing in underground sewers and eating rats.

Both were from very wealthy families and arrived in England with virtually nothing except a few contacts.

Mr Gortway (Stephen) eventually worked his way up and owned a factory in south London making spark plugs. He was awarded the OBE for his services to industry.

Mrs Gortway (Etta) was a very glamorous woman who lived the life of a wealthy lady, chauffeur, mink coats diamonds, shopping at Harrods and playing bridge.

I grew very fond of Mrs Gortway. I became one of the family (well in an employee employer way) they paid for private dental treatment for me and they owned a hairdressers in the village, so free haircuts too, plus holiday pay and bonuses. My job was to go in and cook them their evening meal clean up and leave.

The money was good I had the kitchen to myself, there was a grand piano in the drawing room to play while I was waiting for the food to cook and no one to bother me. Mrs G would come in for a chat and we had quite a few giggles over the years she would confide in me often and we became friends. This temporary job lasted for four and a half years!

It was terrific experience for me. I learned to cook all the Austro Hungarian favourites. They had accounts at all the best shops in Wimbledon village and at Harrods. I could phone up and order what I liked as there was no budget to work to. So I always had the best ingredients to cook with.

Eventually I would cook for their son Andrew and daughter in law Judy who lived in a separate flat at the top of the house as well.

Then when they realised I was good, I was catering for the ladies who lunch, plus some very smart evening dinner parties too. So my job description grew a lot over the years but I didn't mind I was happy there.

They also got me private work where I would do canapés and lunch functions for the Russian Embassy. It was the time of the cold war coming to an end. There was a little mews house in Pimlico where meetings were held supposedly to discuss swopping art and building relations between the two countries. That's all I know. I turned up and did the job.

When I left there in the evenings I would walk around to the Dog and Fox and do a 7 hour shift behind the bar getting in at 3am or later, not every night but at least 3 nights a week. Sometimes I would do a lunchtime session 10.30am until 3pm if they were short staffed or extra busy.

I stayed at the Dog and Fox for about two years but eventually the hours got a bit much. Plus the manager Ken Bridge was a bit of a slave driver and temperamental as hell, yelling his head off etc.

Often we would stay behind after working all night and help him decorate the room for a function, get tables laid up, put decorations up. He was always lavish with the decor, a gay former window dresser with a great eye.

Halloween came and we worked until the early hours getting the bar ready with huge dummies covered in cob webs hanging from the ceiling across the dance floor and witches hiding behind doors, the place looked fabulous. We didn't get paid for any of this so this particular Halloween I said Ken can you pay for a taxi for a few of us to get home? It's freezing outside. I lived about 2 miles down the other end of Wimbledon as did some of the others. He said "no! fucking walk" So I did and never went back.

The Dog and Fox though at that time was a brilliant place to go. The Gay nights Wednesdays started as the Wimbledon Area Gay Society WAGS, (this was a time when outside central London there was nothing for gay people to do or places to meet). It became very trendy and spread to "SUNDAYS" as it was known. If I wasn't working I'd be the other side of the bar with Swales and Colin.

Swales and I would strut our stuff on the dance floor to all the high energy songs of the day sharing bottles of poppers with the likes of Freddie Mercury and Kenny Everett who were regulars too and we had some of the best looking men in London around us. Most weeks there would be a live singer. This would be a popular high energy music star of the time. Hazel Dean, Miquel Brown all of them appeared there promoting "searching" or "so many men so little time" Even the weather girls "I'ts raining men" Fabulous it was.

Swales when he'd had about three or four Carlsberg special brews with large brandies in them! and inhaled a lot of poppers, had a habit of taking all of his clothes off. Usually down to a jock strap showing all of his arse off. Sometimes naked.

One particular night there was a singer on called Erlene Bentley, she had a big hit at the time with "I'm living my own life" A very large black American lady, she was giving it her all on a portable stage to a backing track. Ken Bridge always lavish had ordered a huge basket of fresh flowers to present to the star. It was so packed he couldn't get through the crowds, so he passed the arrangement through the crowd down towards the front.

Unfortunately Swales right near the front, starkers, got hold of it and as Miss Bentley was taking her bows to screams for more, he threw the basket at her saying "here we are love I think these are for you" As she put out her arms to catch it she lost her footing and went arse over tit legs in the air off of the back of the stage.

We were in hysterics. Suddenly we heard Ken Bridge yelling who did that? Who is responsible for this, I'll kill him! I grabbed Swales and we hid behind a curtain until the furore had died down.

Ken never minded Swales getting naked, when he knew it was him he'd say "oh that's only Swales, take no notice."

I'm glad to report Swales did grow out of this Naturist prank.

33

THE 21 CLUB BRIXTON

One of our favourite haunts in those days was the 21 Club. It was situated under a Greek kebab house in Tulse Hill Brixton. It was supposed to be the bar for the restaurant but it was run illegally as a private members club.

Small and cozy the Greek/Cypriot owners had let three gay guys take the basement bar over as a club. This was Peter, Aiden and Tony. Tony I knew from the early Brighton days, he was short, cute and funny and he called everybody "Girl" "yes girl no girl really girl."

They all lived together in a council flat off of the Railton road in Brixton. Railton Road at that time was more famous for the riots. It was known as the front line for the troubles. It wasn't for sissies.

They were all known collectively as the Lickits! Peter Lickit started it off. If you asked for something he didn't have behind the bar or were cheeky instead of telling you to fuck off he'd always say "lick it dear" So did the others.

They were great hosts and as well as fun nights at the club there were often parties at the flat off Railton Road. These were well attended.

One night I saw Tony Lickit stomping about in a bit of a rage. I said what's the matter Tony? He said "I'm furious girl, someone's only gone and pissed in my wardrobe girl" I said oh that's terrible, He said "yes girl the cunts only pissed all over my new duvet, I had it rolled up in the bottom, my mum bought me that for Christmas girl" I had to bite my lip.

Another party there and Colin missed the ship for two days. They had laced the ice trays with poppers, (amyl nitrate) everyone was out of it including our friend Patsy's mum who was well into her 60's.

They had a range of customers at the club, mostly gay, but as always there were a few straight girls and couples in the mix. Predominantly a lot of the Vauxhall tavern crew including Chipmunk and Robert. (Chipmunk had met Robert a year after we met and they are still together to this day as well.)

So it was all quite innocent. I had even taken my great aunt Nel there and Colin's mum when they were staying. They both enjoyed it a lot. So we were totally amazed when one night a load of police in full riot gear charged down the stairs, about 12 of them. This copper who was in charge shouted out "right what's everyone drinking in here then" Chipmunk always quick off the mark said "Cheers dear mines a gin and Tonic", and we all fell about laughing.

Talk about over reaction. There were petrol bombs being hurled at the police at the bottom of the road and they were more worried about a few old poufs having a drink after time.

Anyway that sounded the death knell for the 21 club they only had a restaurant licence so they were in the wrong, but it wasn't doing anyone any harm and it actually made a lot of money for the Greek owners.

A Couple of swells

Colin and me battersea

Me and Colin Wedding 1980

Me at 19

Peter Lickit 21 club Brixton

Ray and Viv Cockney night

Rosina me and Maisie

Viv and Wonderwoman Cricketers

Worse for wear Fuengirola

34

CHAZ N DAVE'S KNEES UP

Work wise things were pretty steady, I was working at the Gortway's. I was always getting called down to Cuckfield by mum to help out when someone was sick or weekends to help with the catering for a wedding or anniversary. Plus I still did the catering for some pub change over parties and played the piano around various pubs in south London. So it was all going ok.

Robert, Chipmunks partner was doing very well. He had worked his way up from a tough background, to owning several nursing homes and was on his way to being a millionaire before he was 40!

I got the catering jobs for the openings of their homes with John Braine doing the flowers. (We always kept it in the family)

Socially the Vauxhall tavern and the Union tavern were still going strong. We got very friendly with a great northern couple called Paul and Nikki James who did cabaret on the gay scene as well as the northern club circuit.

Peter Stringfellow opened the Hippodrome in the old home of The Talk of the Town in the west end and Nicki and Paul James were booked as top of the bill on Monday the gay night. We had a great moment when we all walked outside to see their names in big lights in the west end. Nikki was so nervous (unusual for her) and kept throwing up in the dressing room. However when they came up through the stage on the hydraulic lift Nicki singing "And I am telling you" from the dream girls, they brought the house down. We went on holidays together and then moved on. They became big on the American cruise ships and eventually we lost touch sadly.

Rosina had managed to get tickets for the filming of the Chaz and Dave Christmas show for ITV. They were huge stars then and number one in the charts with "There ain't no pleasin you" which we all loved and she took me, Chipmunk and Swales with her to see it.

We were disappointed when we got there, as we were allocated seats in the audience where you had to watch everyone on the set having a good time. ITV had built a London pub from scratch in the studios and Chaz n Dave invited all their friends and families plus theatrical extras to have a Christmas knees up.

We found it torture sitting there watching them all having a drink and a party without being able to join in. Chaz had a bottle of brandy under the piano and the others looked like they were drinking real beer. So when nobody was looking we crept down the aisle and jumped over the security barrier and walked straight up to the bar, trying to blend in. The barman took one look at me and said "fuck me Jeremy what are you doing here?" it turned out to be an old pal from Brighton I'd not seen for years. I said Shh don't say anything just give us all a drink. He said you're the only ones in here without stage makeup on your going to get caught. Well we didn't we had a blast. We partied all night with Eric Clapton, Jim Davidson, Peters and lee and others plus Chaz n Dave themselves. You can still see us on clips on you tube. It was the number one Christmas show that year with millions of viewers. Fame at last!

35

YUPPIES

There was a burst of excitement in the 1980's, money was not a problem for a lot of people although remained hard for some, especially in the north. Margaret Thatcher had revolutionised the city of London. Now barrow boys could become hedge fund managers. Social class didn't matter anymore, ability did. It took a Conservative Prime minister to achieve this, Labour never did. It didn't matter what your background was, if you were prepared to work hard and take a few risks the world was your oyster.

Lots of people became shareholders. People bought their council houses thanks to Maggie's right to buy scheme and were able to climb the property ladder instead of being stuck on sink estates for the rest of their lives.

Joan Collins swished about in TV's Dynasty with huge padded shoulders, JR was outmanoeuvring everyone in TV's Dallas and glamour was in the air.

After the depressing 1970's recession, filled with anger and daily strikes, things were looking up. There was an entrepreneurial atmosphere. The word Yuppie was coined which meant anyone (mainly in the city) aspiring to be rich. They clutched a thick filofax in one hand and a mobile phone the size of a house brick in the other.

The exception was the miner's strike which was terrible and caused lots of resentment on both sides. The trade unionist Arthur

Scargill used the miners to have one last attempt to bring the country to its knees, but eventually he lost as did a lot of poor mining communities whose pits were closed down. Harold Wilson the Labour PM had actually closed more pits down than Mrs Thatcher but she will always be remembered for it. However she did manage to smash the unions iron grip over everything and things got better. However it wasn't good for everyone, her monetarist policies had caused a lot of misery and hardship for people to. But basically she got the country out of debt.

My parents left the Talbot in Cuckfield after 10 years where they had made lots of friends and were given a very warm, generous and emotional send off by the customers.

After a mini break they became the new licensees of a private members club in upmarket Rottingdean an old English village 6 miles east of Brighton.

36

THE ROTTINGDEAN CLUB PART ONE

So in 1984 my family moved to Rottingdean. The Club was and still is an historical and beautiful building.

Situated towards the top of the village near the pond, it was the only licensed premises in the village to have a garden. A very nice one too. There are also 5 pubs in Rottingdean.

It had been part of the hotel which adjoined it at the time called the 'Old Place hotel'. The middle section was originally two old fishermen's cottages rumoured to be dating back to the 1300's the rest of the building was 15-1600's. The outside was built of flint stones originally hauled up from the beach. Inside there were 3 linked sections and in some parts very low ceilings and old oak beams.

In the 1960's it had been sold off by the hotel I guess to raise some money. However part of it had been used as a private club since the 1940's.

Eventually Watney's brewery bought it and put in managers. This worked for a while but it wasn't taking much money.

My parents were offered this as a bribe to get them out of the Talbot which they said they wanted to close and redevelop as offices. (They never did)

My parents told them that they would only consider it if

Watney's created a tenancy agreement for them, where they would pay them a rent for the building but any money was theirs.

This was agreed and we took over. Change over days back then were crazy. You would have one family moving out while the other moved in. The bar was kept open and local publicans from around the area would pop in to wish you luck and spend lots of money, so that you would start off your first day with a good days takings in the till.

Hard to be sociable, work and designate where to put your furniture, drink non stop and be merry all at the same time. We played it down this time, remembering back to the Talbot change-over which was hectic, where mum had made trays of cottage pies before we left London and which were in the boot of the old Morris minor to put on the lunch menu from day one!

This time a barman did the lunchtime, we got moved in upstairs, unpacking boxes as they came in and got beds made up etc.

So I was the first one in the family to pull a pint there. I actually opened up at 6pm.

Some of the locals came in to have a good look of course but I think I made a good impression.

This club was meant to be a bit of a slower pace for my folks as they were in their mid 50's in 1984. However within two weeks we were really busy. Mum had started making a few of her famous steak and kidney pies and the word went round the village. Even then only one pub in the village was doing lunches, The Plough opposite. It was planned for one of our loyal old staff Enid to run the bar at lunchtimes and do a few snacks on her own. That didn't last long. Soon it was all systems go and we were doing up to 70-100 lunches a day.

We were allowed to have 1000 members by law and we got around this by adding 'A' numbers for partners on joint memberships. So we had about 1600-2 thousand members in a short time.

There was a committee there as it was a club and whilst co-operating to an extent, they had to be told that it was no longer a managed private club but a private business. This of course put a few noses out of joint but my parents were paying all the bills so they were not going to be told how to run their own business. They found that out on the first meeting with my Mother. So it was changed into an entertainments committee for a few years and eventually phased out completely.

I loved the club, the people were nice on the whole and most importantly very good drinkers.

The downside of the club was it didn't have a catering kitchen, there was a small kitchen behind the bar. Two of you in there and it was a crowd. There was no window either just an old extractor fan. So it got very hot and difficult to work in but we did. I spent a lot of my free time there over the next 18 months. Mum started doing the odd function so I would be called down to help. We used to set up paint tables down in the cellars. They were good big cellars, one with a cold room which was great for storage. We would stand down there for hours on hard concrete floors making salads, cutting up meats, racing upstairs to the oven down again to plate up. We made everything ourselves and never bought in.

John Braine got roped in again to do the flowers if it was a wedding. He would go to New Covent Garden for the flowers and bring them down on the train.

We built up trade with the fun nights and massive BBQs in the summers that were always sold out.

On summers nights tired out you could walk down to the pretty beach and soak your feet in the sea at midnight.

One day I got a call from Mum saying that one of the area managers had popped in and asked how I was. He said "has Jeremy ever considered taking over his own pub?" She said "I don't know" He said "I've got a little pub come up in Brighton near the Theatre Royal it needs someone with a bit of flair to take it over and build it up"

I spoke to Colin about it and although he wasn't keen, he thought it would be good for me.

So I rang the brewery and said yes. By then we had started

socialising again in Brighton. I had taken Colin down years before to meet Terrie Varley and she had approved. Brighton was on an upswing and the gay pub scene was improving and we had made very good friends with a couple of publicans called Tracy and John Davenport who owned the Queens arms in George Street.

Colin loved Brighton, London had started to go down a bit, although Lily Savage had started packing them in at the Vauxhall, other places like the Union tavern, the Market tavern, the Copacabana club had all closed down.

It was a bit stale, so my contact at the brewery said it was just a formality but we would have to go down for an interview but could we move quickly. So I handed in my notice at the Gortways who were devastated I was leaving, I cancelled a bit of work I had lined up under my "Puddings" title, had the interview and started packing.

About two weeks later I got a phone call from Terrie Varley and she said, "I don't know how to tell you this but you haven't got that pub your after" I said don't be daft they asked me to take it, I'm nearly packed and ready to move. She told me who had told her and it was a reliable source. I rang the brewery and was told yes I'm afraid so Jeremy we've given it to somebody else, somebody more local, I shouted, more local! I know everyone in Brighton you idiots. I said don't you think you could have phoned me first. I was so upset.

I had big plans for this bar and had lots of contacts on the entertainment scene in London I could bring down to offer something Brighton didn't have then. I wanted a piano cabaret bar and knew all the best acts.

When I told my mother she was so mad she jumped in a taxi straight away barged into this man's office in Brighton and gave him it with both barrels.

Years later I was to get my sweet revenge, I'll tell you how further on.

My sister gave birth to my first nephew and mum and dad's first grandchild Jonothan O'Connor. I was more or less present at the birth, pacing up and down outside with a bottle of champagne and glasses. I found it all quite emotional. Holding him for the first time I felt bonded straight away and understood the saying blood is thicker than water. I was around for the first few months of his life before mine changed and it was great taking part in that.

So what to do now? after the initial shock had worn off mum rang and said "don't unpack everything, look for a flat down here and you can take over the catering at the Rottingdean club make it your own business" I was dubious, she said "I could use a break from that side for a while, move down, you have that bit of the business and we'll keep the bar side. It doesn't have to be forever, just until another pub comes up. Besides you're in a rut up there with your little jobs you need to start thinking about building a bigger career" Mum also very generously offered to lend us a deposit to put down on a flat if we could get a mortgage. It was a gamble but we took it. With a deposit of £3.000 we managed to buy our first owned home at 83a Queens Park Road Brighton. It wasn't without its dramas, off one minute on the next but we did it.

Just before we moved back to Brighton I was in a Club in Streatham one night where I bumped in to two old friends. David Raven aka Maisie Trollette and Chris Darnell (Maggie) who had been the manager of the Union Tavern in Camberwell and the Vauxhall Tavern for a while. They said we are both moving to Brighton, Maisie or David as he prefers had bought a guest house called Roland House in Kemp Town and Chris had bought a pub (The Aquarium in Steine Street). I said I'm moving down there too. We all had a laugh about it, we all moved to Brighton within three days of each other and a whole new in Brighton's gay scene was about to begin.

Cary grant news of the world

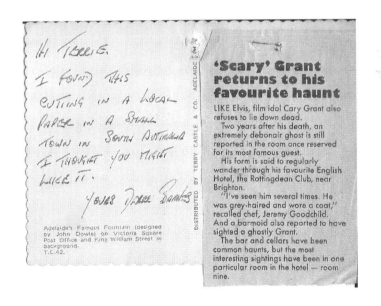

Cary grant

Don Mine Host

Family xmas Rottingdean club

Garden at the rottingdean club

Me mum and john Wedding we had prepared.

Phantom of the opera night

Rottingdean club

Ve day mum and dad

We loved to Sing

37

Brighton revisited

It all worked very well, we moved in December 1986 people said it never snows in Brighton. Well that year it did, we had the heaviest snowfall in years! The boiler broke down, not what you need when you first move in!

Luckily Colin's brother in law Geoff was handy like that and installed a new one for us.

In 1987 we had the famous hurricane too. The house rocked literally and a split came down the centre of the building. So many trees were killed and strewn across the road. We had never seen anything like it in the south. I still managed to get in to work, there was no electricity so I improvised a cold menu by candlelight to feed all the people who didn't go to work, and we were busy. There was a bit of a British gung ho atmosphere and after lunch I got on the piano in the bar and we all had a sing song. Very Blitz spirit it was.

The new property was super. A three bedroom maisonette on three levels with its own street entrance. A bathroom with a huge corner bath (all the rage in the 80's) Big Victorian rooms, an enormous kitchen and sitting room. I had to pinch myself, we were living in such luxury and it was all ours, a great feeling. We could never have afforded it in London.

Within days I had taken over the catering at the Rottingdean club. The hours were great 10am until 3pm Monday to Saturday.

We didn't do dinner then so I was able to be home by 4pm. The hours were short but it was very busy and it was not unusual to do 45-70 lunches between 12.30 and 2pm so it was full on.

Originally I just did my mother's menu which was basically hot pies, savoury 'jacket' potatoes and sandwiches. Once I settled in I extended this menu a lot and did a full menu with about 15 different choices each day. I prepared, cooked and served all the food myself with one assistant to wash up in a tiny windowless kitchen, the heat was a killer.

The business increased further and the takings went up.

I paid my own staff and bought my own stock. I had the odd bad week as well as good but I was making good money.

Colin and I went a bit mad the first 6 months. The novelty of moving to Brighton with so much going on within walking distance was too tempting for words. We were out most nights. Eventually this had to stop as we had permanent hangovers and it's not fun cooking in a really hot kitchen feeling like death warmed up.

Still we made up for it at the weekends and only one or two nights out during the week. Sunday was the big day in Brighton, it still is!

Our house was open house, but we would start at a designated pub usually the Queens arms in George Street, (Tracy's) or the Bedford Tavern in Western St was another Sunday favourite. There we would meet up with friends for a drink. After the pubs closed at 2pm! (Which they had to by law then) we would head off to the Longbranch private members club in Grand Parade and drink until 4pm. The Longbranch was run by two lesbians called Roz and Peggy. They were not the most cheerful people in the world. The carpet on the bar floor was so covered in booze that your feet literally stuck to the carpet. Roz used to stand on the door like a prison warden in Cell block H.

After the club whoever was staying with us and whoever had joined the company would head back to our house in Queens Park Road where I would have prepared a big Sunday roast, enough for an army. Because pubs had to close at 2pm and stay closed until 7pm on Sundays, no pubs served lunch, it wasn't worth it. Seems strange now but that's how it was. I think it was better. The atmosphere in the pubs Sunday lunchtime was great. Lots of drinks, banter and no screaming kids running around.

Sometimes I'd have 8-10 people for lunch, most weeks in fact. After lunch we would gather around the piano for a singsong or listen to records. Then everyone would find somewhere to have a doze then we would get up go out and do it all again. We also had lots of big parties too and we were well known for our Boxing Day bash which were always great fun. David Raven used to bring the whole family from Roland House.

After the Queens arms closed at 10.30pm we went onto the Longbranch club again! (It had a midnight license) then at midnight we would go off to a licensed gay hotel for a lock in. They were supposed to be serving guests only so it was all a bit hush hush. One night there was a police raid and about 40 of us had to cram in this back kitchen room, the scullery. I can remember all of us trying not to laugh in case the police heard us and trying not to be sick as there were stacks of empty kitikat tins lined up on the draining board, it stunk. I don't think they served it for breakfast.

Another night leaving there I couldn't get a taxi. This guy offered me a lift so I said thanks I only live up the road but it's very steep and I'm freezing. "I'll take you on my bike he said" I was looking around for a Harley Davidson or something, pointing he said "no that's it" It was a fold up mobyallete chained to the lamp post. I said I can't get on that! Worrying about my street cred, he said "you will if you want to get home" Anyway I climbed on shivering. I was wearing this black Lurex jacket with huge padded shoulders with a big diamante brooch on the lapel ala Joan Collins) (excuse me it was the 1980's and that was how we all dressed) anyway he unfolded and started this thing up and off we went.

We got to the top of the first hill, Upper rock gardens and we hear a police car behind us with its siren on. They pulled us over in

Egremont place (known as Vaseline alley because a lot of gay men lived there) and breathalysed him, he was ok but I was pissed and had been singing Gracie Fields "Sally" at the top of my voice. I got done for not wearing a helmet, aiding and abetting a learner driver, (how did I know) fined, and 3 penalty points on my licence. (Don't you just hate the police sometimes?)

Most weekends we had guests from London. It happens when you move to the seaside. I never minded they were all welcome. Chipmunk and Robert, Swales, John Braine, the Baron were all regulars. We had plenty of room and we all loved a party. When I look back I don't know how I did it. I was cooking 6 days a week and then again on Sunday for all my friends. TerrieVarley came most Sundays for years. I was young so you don't care.

There was no entertainment in the gay pubs in Brighton in those days, Cabaret hadn't arrived. I remember Morag the Scottish barman in the Queens arms miming in the corner with a mop head on his head miming to chain reaction by Diana Ross. I said to Tracy and John you can do better than this. The Queens arms wasn't a gay pub then, it had a busy lunchtime trade from American Express in Edward Street and at night a mixed clientele.

(Morag the lovely Jim was savagely murdered a few years later, beaten around the head with a hammer. He was a lovely man much loved and it shocked the community greatly)

At Camp Camp with John and Swales

Barry Barrington

Dennis Egan and Jean H

Jean Hirigoyen and i presentation
for Terrie Varleys 70th

Eartha Kitt at Camp Camp with Adrella Skegness

In benidorm with Terrie V, Tracy Donna John H

Jean Hirigoyen and Terrie Varley

Lily Savage (Paul O'Grady) hungover at Camp Camp

On stage somewhere having a good time

Peter Stanford Dockyard Doris Maisie Trollette John Bruzon Fudges

Phil Star at Fudges

Queens park road

The Baron David Raven Gibralter Airport

Typical sunday afternoon at QP

The Baron Jack and John

With Miss Jason at Brighton Pride.

With Scott st Martyn Sitges

38

TRACY (ANN ROGERS) DAVENPORT

We all loved Tracy because she was glamorous, extremely kind and warm, funny and beautiful.

She was an ex actress and singer. She had had a successful career in the 1960's in films, television and recordings. She appeared in some really good films Like 'The leather boys' with Rita Tushingham and 'what a crazy World' with Joe Brown and Mary Wilde plus a who's who of British actors of the time.

Noel Coward had chosen her straight out of Italia Conte stage school to fly to New York to appear in 'The Girl who came to supper' with Tessie O'Shea. She had to be chaperoned by her mother. She was Britain's answer to Brigitte Bardot. She appeared on stage with Anthony Newley in Stop the world I want to get off. She had a number one hit record with the theme from Love Story a popular 1970's TV series. Tracy released 7 singles on the Polydor label owned by her future husband and had endless TV credits and pantomimes to her name. She knew everyone, was great pals with Joan Collins when Joan was married to Newley and she was very modest about all this and hardly spoke about it.

Now she is the landlady of our favourite pub 'The Queens Arms' along with her colourful husband John (JD) (Dolly) Davenport. Chalk and cheese they were. John was a bit of a south London rough diamond. He had had several pubs. He met Tracy at a pub changeover party in Mitcham Surrey. (I have no idea why she was there) He had a way with words, lots of patter, and was very funny, they got on like a house on fire. They eloped there and then to Brighton (both were married). Turning up with what they wore on their backs to a friend's house and never looked back.

After a successful run at another pub they took over the tenancy of the QA in the early 1980's. Although running successfully Tracy and John liked to spend their free time in the gay pubs and clubs. With Tracy's theatrical background she was a natural and was eventually adored by the gay community. So they decided to turn the Queens arms into a gay bar. Paul from Cuckfield introduced me to Tracy just like he had to the Curtain Club all of those years ago.

I was in turn able to introduce Tracy to people like David Raven (Maisie Trollette) and la Cage Aux Folles star Scott st Martyn and Brighton legends like Terrie Varley. Soon there were proper cabaret acts appearing at the Queens Arms and it was amongst the first in Brighton to do so. It was a huge success. The gay community took Tracy and John to their hearts and the place was packed out every night.

One Monday afternoon I got a phone call from David Raven (Maisie Trollette) "What are you doing tonight?" Me; Nothing I've really hurt my back I can hardly move. "Well you'll have to move. I've taken a booking at the Queens arms tonight and I can't get a pianist. So darling I was wondering if you would be an angel and come down and play for me". Me "no I'm sorry I can't I really am in agony and anyway that piano in there hasn't been tuned". Tracy and John had acquired it when a pub at the top of the road (The Ranleigh) had gone bust. They got a couple of blokes to wheel it down St James Street getting the Loud/ continuation peddle knocked off in the process.

"Oh go on said David a few drinks you'll be ok and I'll make sure there's a comfortable chair with cushions. Please Jeremy it's only this once I promise"

I gave in of course. The piano was terrible, the whole act was off the cuff and it went down very well. They plied me with Brandy and we did over an hour.

This eventually went on for nearly two years. Maisie could always pull a big crowd but this was a bit different and something worked. Maybe people liked to see me working as the stooge. One night he said to me on the stage in front of the crowd. "Jeremy has been so good to me, he plays that dreadful piano, puts up with my jokes and my ways, has been a good friend through thick and thin" etc etc. So he said "I want you to come up on stage as I've got a present for you". He said "we asked Colin what you would really really like as a present and he said you would give anything to see Frank Sinatra, Liza Minnelli and Sammy Davis Jr at the Albert hall in Concert is that right darling? "Yes I said flabbergasted I would" "Well because you've been so kind to me I've got hold of some tickets and I want you to have them as a thank you. Please accept these with my thanks." Emotional as I went to take the envelope he threw it up into the air when dozens of bits of paper flew out into the audience and he said "and if any other silly fucker's stupid enough to believe that want to go too, here you are here's the rest !"

Well the place erupted. People had tears pouring down their faces, me included. It sounds really cruel, but he was only having a joke. He was always a practical joker as anyone who's been on holiday with him will vouch for. His specialities are;

Hiding in the wardrobe to hand you a shirt as you opened the door, hiding under the bed and when you got in and laid down, an arm would come up from under the bed and grab you, you get the picture.

We used to double up those Monday nights and then go up to Villagers club at the top of St James Street and do another show there to. They had a proper concert grand so I was able to show those still sober enough I didn't always sound like Les Dawson on speed.

The piano at the Queens arms because the pedals wouldn't work had to be played hard for volume and quickly to try and hide the gaps between the notes. Some nights my fingers used to bleed literally.

They were happy times and David was always generous with me. He used to split the fee 50/50 which he didn't have to do and I saved that money and went on a dream holiday with John Braine to New York, San Francisco, Hollywood and Las Vegas. Not many had done those sorts of trips then and it was very glamorous and exciting.

Tracy

Tracy Davenport nee(Ann) Tracy Rogers

39

Viva Las Vegas

Las Vegas sticks in my mind because once we got over the glamour of it we decided to check out the gay bars. Using the Bob Damron international gay guide we located a bar on Liberace drive. This turned out to be a seedy side of town but even in there there were gambling machines bedded into the bar counter. We ordered a drink and then the barman came up and said to us. 'I can tell you are not from around here, I'm going to call you a taxi, there are some rough types in here eyeing you up, I suggest you go some-where safer" Which was really nice of him. So we got into the taxi and asked the driver to take us to a gay nightclub.

We seemed to drive for quite a distance and eventually we saw this neon sign in the distance. "That's it over there" said the driver. After we paid him and walked towards the bar we noticed that the neon sign was hanging off a bit. Alert but not perturbed (we had been around Vauxhall often enough after all) Inside it was quite nice but, we were the only men. It was a Lesbians bar.

Anyway, we sat at the bar and watched the butch barmaid mix these exotic looking cocktails. "Whad'll you have guys?" she said. I said (my voice had gone very high pitched) we'll have two of those please, what are they? "Out here we call em Cowboy Cocksuckers honey!" Just then this other woman next to me slid off her bar-stool and crawling on her hands and knees started yelling Barbara Barbara give me some drugs. "Pipe down Mary" said the barmaid.

"Cant you see I'm fucking busy" She gave us our drinks. I said I think we've come to the wrong bar. She laughed out loud, you sure have honey. I said don't worry we will drink these and go. "I'll call you a cab honey" No its ok please don't bother we will walk. She gave me an odd look and shrugged her shoulders. We downed our cowboy cocksuckers in one go and headed out the door in hysterics. We started to walk, we thought we'll just flag a cab down, by now it was pitch black outside. Well we walked and walked for about an hour. We had no idea if we were going in the right direction or not. We were in the middle of the Nevada dessert. Getting a bit worried now we were a bit frightened, when all of a sudden in the distance we saw a cars headlights coming towards us. Thank God we both said. Eventually it got close enough to see but we thought it must be a mirage because it was a black London taxi with the hire light on. (I swear on my mother's life) He pulled up and a Cockney voice said "where are you going mate?" We couldn't believe it. He heard our accents and said "I bet you never expected to see a cockney cab driver out here in the middle of the dessert did you?" No we didn't I replied but never have I been so glad to see one. It turned out he had retired out there and had the cab shipped over. He did quite a good business because of the novelty factor.

40

Brighton Aid

In the 1980's the terrible disease Aids raised its ugly head. It was very prevalent in the gay community in the USA and the UK. There was also an epidemic of it in Africa amongst straight people, but in the UK the press named it the "Gay Plague" and tortured anyone famous who contracted the disease. People like Rock Hudson and Freddie Mercury. Overnight it seemed to appear. It was a terminal disease and involved a long slow death.

You started to notice people in pubs looking dreadfully thin, we thought it was cancer. Eventually many of our friends succumbed to this awful disease and we lost lots of them. It was heartbreaking to watch friends become skeletons covered with sores and die far too young.

No one knew where it had come from. It was rumoured that it was spread by monkeys and that someone had had sex with a monkey and eventually the disease spread to humans. Others said it was germ warfare gone wrong. That the Americans had developed it as a weapon against Vietnam and had used a little to test it and it had spread.

These were all rumours and there never was any evidence to back it up. Other's said it was spread by promiscuity which is true but promiscuity did not invent it, but unprotected sex and blood contact did help spread it, but people didn't know. After years of repression for gay people the new relaxed atmosphere, although still illegal under 21 in the UK, led to a surge in gay sex clubs where sex was available everywhere, people went a bit mad and there was a Babylon atmosphere.

Now 40 years on there is still no cure, but it is not the death sentence it once was if caught in time.

So taking the bull by the horns the gay community started having fund raisers and charity nights and collections in all of the clubs and Pubs in London.

Millions of pounds were raised and 'The Terrence Higgins Trust' was set up an organisation to treat, look after and advise people with HIV and Aids.

Down in Brighton I noticed that nothing was being done. Brighton had the largest gay community outside of London but nobody seemed to have taken much notice. Gay pubs were still generous as ever but raising money for blind dogs and Lifeboats. Nothing wrong with that of course, it's very noble, but when your own community is being ravaged by a killer disease your priority should be that.

I was mentioning this in conversation to John and Tracy one day in the bar. So John Davenport said to me, "alright we will start it in here at the Queens Arms. You organise it Jeremy and we will back you up" Chipmunk and Robert were with me and Robert wrote out a cheque for £50 and said there you go that's to start you off. £50 was a very generous donation then.

So that's what happened. I wrote to all the gay Pubs and Clubs in Brighton and asked if they would be willing to have a meeting with me in the Queens arms to discuss ways to raise money to support the Aids charities.

The response was phenomenal. All but one or two responded positively and wanted to get involved. I said it would work better if we all worked together as we would raise more money that way. Petty feuds were put aside and the community came together.

We decided we didn't want a committee as such (although myself and Tracy were appointed treasurers) we wanted to work together as a Cooperative. Which meant everyone got involved and had a say in how to do things. We wanted to keep it informal and friendly. However without a chairman it can get tricky when people disagree over something, but a majority vote usually sorted things out.

We were all naive in how to do this but on the whole it worked very well. We decided to meet each week in one of the bars, everyone taking it in turns to host.

So that night the first Aids fundraising charity in Brighton was born. We called ourselves Brighton Aid.

The Brighton Aid Ball

Tony Chapman (Moisha) the owner of the Beacon Royal gay hotel and nightclub said we could use his premises for our first event. We decide to start big and organise a Ball.

Those of us with contacts in show business were able to contact acts to ask if they would come and appear for free.

We got a good cast together of local acts, singers comics, drag artists, A top high energy singer of the time and top of the bill Was Paul O'Grady as Lily Savage with Skippy (his glove puppet made out of an old fox fur from a charity shop). There are clips of this on you tube today.

I compared the show that night along with Richard one of the owners of 'The Villagers club' in Kemp Town. It was hugely successful. All the staff worked for nothing that night and put their wages into the fund which was lovely of them. As well as ticket sales we were given items of antique furniture and jewellery to auction from generous benefactors, which we did in the dining room of the hotel. In total we raised just over a staggering £14,000 that night. In the 80's it was huge.

We were all amazed at the success but it just encouraged us to do more. Throughout the year most of the bars had fundraisers and raffles and people donated money in bucket collections.

Towards the end of the year we threw another Ball at the Beacon Royal this time a Beau Arts Ball. Same formula as before but this time with the lovely Su Pollard topping the bill. We raised over £7,000 on this occasion to.

So now we had to decide how to spend the money. We wanted it to go to local people with HIV and Aids and to actually buy things for them they really wanted.

The first place we went to was the Aids wing at the Royal Sussex county hospital in Brighton. A small delegation of us went. We were very shocked when we got there. There were skull and crossbones posters on the doors saying stay out! We had to wear protective clothing before we could enter. This was a long time before Princess Diana famously shook hands and hugged that gay man in London. The fear back then was extraordinary but understandable.

After going around the beds and chatting to the guys in there it seemed that the things they lacked were little things like electric razors which made shaving for those who had lost weight easier. Kettles so they could make a cup of tea. They needed televisions and things that would help pass the time.

With a list of these items Tracy and I were able to go to Curry's electric suppliers and buy up lots of razors, kettles, televisions and a couple of video recorders. Plus any personal items the guys needed.

They were so grateful it was heartbreaking they really were the outcasts, treated like lepers with very little outside contact.

We had secret meetings a couple of times at Villagers in the afternoons. Richard and Tony the owners got very friendly with a couple of the doctors and they came in to meet some of us to discuss this epidemic.

They told us there was a government cover up going on and it would only get worse and far from it being a gay plague it was now spreading everywhere and affecting all people from all walks of life. The biggest increase at that time was in women, mainly in Africa. The situation seemed hopeless with no light at the end of the tunnel.

I'm sorry to say that Richard and Tony both succumbed to this disease themselves eventually. They were hugely popular amongst the gay community in Brighton and they played a big hand in raising money and awareness.

Brighton Aid was never meant to be a long term project and after 2 years we wrapped it up. We were able to help a lot of people in that time. With anything from funeral costs to new beds. There had been a bit of nasty gossip from one or two about where the money was going etc.

Colin and I had bought a cheap second hand car with our own money and Tracy went to Benidorm with the Varley tours brigade a couple of times again with her own hard earned money. We heard that some people were saying I bet we paid for that etc. Luckily we had kept receipts and books for every item ever purchased and published an article in a gay paper to invite people to come and inspect the accounts and have a look if they liked. Nobody did.

This sort of thing goes on I know but after all the work we had put in and lots of our own money we had had enough.

So we were able to hand the balance of the funds over to a new fundraising group called Brighton Cares to help set up the first aids hospice in Brighton called The Sussex Beacon. We closed the bank account. Everyone kept up with the fundraising.

I'm very proud of what we achieved. From nothing to £14,000 on the first big night and lots more. A letter from me brought the gay business community together for the first time. We helped an awful lot of people who had nobody to turn to, and we created an environment where fundraising prospered and grew.

David Raven at 85 and the other acts are still raising money for the Sussex beacon now.

41

HAPPY DAYS

Besides the sadness of the Aids epidemic there was also a lot of fun to be had in the late 80's and early 1990s and we took full advantage of it.

Work was good, I was working hard at the club; I took on lots of private functions, weddings, funerals, birthday parties. We did seem to do lots of funerals. Big affairs too. Often members left money in their wills so that they could have their wake at the Rottingdean Club. These were hard work but profitable. One day we did three weddings on one day. Two in the club and one to take away to an outside venue + about 70 lunches.

I did all the food myself with help from my mother. Hours and hours we stood on hard concrete floors preparing salmons in aspic, seafood platters, roast ribs of beef, ham on the bone, homemade pies and quiches and always about 10 fresh salads to choose from plus Trifles and Gateaux's. We did buy the Puddings in but that was all. Sometimes people just wanted endless trays of sandwiches or canapés. More hard work I used to think with all the different fillings.

We used to dress the tables elaborately with freshly starched linen, fresh flowers and ribbons, used the best silverware and glass where possible to.

All these functions plus the normal lunches and everyday business.

Some of the funerals were more fun than the weddings. I've lost count on how many but it was literally many hundreds I should think.

My social life didn't slow down either. I still held open house most Sundays and I did this for 10 years.

Brighton cares (the charity we handed our Brighton aid balance to) was the sister of West End Cares. Both put on huge benefit nights throughout this period in London and in Brighton.

The London affairs were magnificent. Big Hollywood stars would join in. My good friend Jae Alexander was often the musical director of these shows. Big lavish productions with just about everybody from the theatre involved.

One night a friend of mine Denis Egan and I went to see ("a night of a hundred stars" Cole Porter's centenary gala) in this were Alice Faye, Bea Arthur, Van Johnson, Adelaide hall, Katherine Grayson and zillions of other names. We went back stage to see a friend of his Broadway star Julie Harris who was in it. While we were waiting to go into the dressing room. We noticed a bit of a row going on at the stage door. It was film star Van Johnson who was a huge man, he was very drunk and yelling "Where's my god damned car" and waving his arms around in a very camp manner.

Next to him was this tiny little old lady wrapped up in a Mac and head scarf tugging at his arm and saying "Now Van stop this nonsense, there is no car, we will have to try and get a cab like everybody else. This was Alice Faye.

It had been a great show and one that helped raised millions for Aids Research.

In Brighton they were smaller affairs held at the Brighton Dome but just as good.

Plenty of British stars got involved as did some of our friends. David Raven as Maisie Trollette of course other well loved drag acts like Phil Starr and Dave Lynn. Tracy made her big stage comeback too.

Once they got her to sing "Any dream will do" from Joseph and his Technicolor raincoat. She had to enter the stage from a platform at a great height; they made her technicolour raincoat out of towelling beer mats as a nod to her landlady status. It was huge and covered a lot of the stage. She had to walk into the coat if you can visualise it. It got a huge round of Applause and Tracy got a well earned standing ovation for her performance.

As well as these benefits I saw nearly every show at the theatre Royal in Brighton as being in business we were advertisers for the theatre. They gave us a free pass for two free tickets each week. It was a good system because if we liked it (us and other Publicans/restaurateurs) we would tell our customers so we helped sell tickets.

As well as the Brighton cares shows Tracey Davenport got together with Scott st Martyn, Dave Lynn and Costume designer Steven Metcalfe to write and put on alternative pantomimes at the Pavilion Theatre.

Some were directed by Dr Who and BBC producers John Nathan Turner and partner Gary Downie who were customers of ours at the club and I was able to introduce them to the Brighton "family" These were cheeky risqué shows and the tickets always sold out like hotcakes.

This hadn't been seen in Brighton since the days of the 42 club. Where owners Syd Lewis and Tony Stuart used to write and produce an annual adult pant, staged at theatres in Brighton. They were always a sell out and people bought tickets months in advance.

Now my friends were reviving the tradition and they proved to be huge success, again raising lots of money for Aids charities.

I used to take a big party to these shows. My mother and several of her girlfriends would get taxis in from Rottingdean and would meet me and Colin plus friends at Barrington's hotel in Grand Parade opposite the Dome.

My friend Barry Barrington owned and ran this hotel with his mother Rene.

Barry was very flamboyant with a huge laugh and sometimes a

terrible hairpiece. He was always immaculately dressed in the best suits and shirts 'Frogget' (Brighton's best men's outfitters) could provide plus lots of jewellery and most of Rene's too.

On these occasions when we were going to a benefit fund raiser and there were many of them then, we would congregate at Barry's for drinks and then go back after the show for a party. Barry used to rope Syd Lewis (42 club) in and Barry Smith (Whites club) to help with the catering and they used to produce some of the most beautiful buffet tables you could imagine.

They were wonderful evenings and much missed.

Barry's other "gift" revolved around men's toilets. He was an ardent "cottager" That's a man who looks for sex in men's toilets. However Barry did it in style. On his day off he would make his way to his favourite "Cottage" and armed with a couple of Rene's mink coats and a few shopping bags, he would get to the gents to stake out his space for the day. He liked to get there in time to catch the commuters and workman on their way to or from work.

He would line the floor with Rene's minks and light scented tea light candles and dot them about and on the cistern. In the bags he used to have 2 flasks one with tea and one with coffee. A bottle of brandy and two cut glass brandy goblets. "One must always be able to offer ones guests refreshments eh?" in a Tupperware dish he would have a few sandwiches (crusts off) smoked salmon or cucumber and a bit of lemon and parsley for garnish plus a packet of wet wipes.

I said to him wryly, "what do you do with the bags?"

He had thought of everything, he said "well dear when a gentleman caller comes in I get him to place a foot in each bag, that way if anyone looks underneath they can only see two feet instead of four!" They were Harrods bags of course.

SYD AND BARRY

Barry Smith was another larger than life character. He lived in the basement flat of a large house in St Aubyns Hove and Syd Lewis of the 42 club lived on the top floor with Tony Stuart.

Barry was very rotund and had the most wonderful facial expressions. He always had a cigarette on and looked and sounded like a disgusted Bette Davis. He was hilarious as well as terribly bitchy. An awful snob he had a very good job at the gentlemen's club in London "Whites" They used to do the outside catering at Ascot whose guests included the Royal family. Princess Margaret would only ever allow Barry to serve her "tea" he used to fill her teapot with Famous Grouse whiskey and top her teacup up with that.

Barry and Syd were friends for years although forever falling out and vowing on their mothers lives to never speak to each other again, until the next time.

Early on in their friendship when funds were low Syd went around the charity shops and managed to get hold of two ladies Salvation Army costumes. Syd altered them to fit him and Barry and donned with suitable wigs and their 'Sally Army' bonnets and tambourines, they boarded a bus to Newhaven.

Once there they would stand outside the pubs singing Salvation Army favourites like 'What a friend we have in Jesus' and 'hand me down my silver trumpet Gabriel' then go around the bar for a collection into their tambourines. One look from Barry and they tipped up.

They would spend the money getting legless once they got back to Brighton.

Syd Lewis was an immensely talented artist, designer and costume maker. He designed the last poster Dorothy Squires ever used for her last live performance at the Brighton Dome.

Barry and Syd

42

CAMP CAMP

Peter Searle a famous London drag queen Adrella, organised what is now a legendary event called Camp Camp it was in the late 1980's and Held at Butlin's holiday camp in Skegness out of season.

Coach loads of gay men and women made their way from London and Brighton to this freezing cold northern resort in March to pay homage to the very successful TV show staring Su Pollard and Ruth Madoc called Hi di Hi set in a holiday camp called 'Maplins' in the 1950's.

A fun packed weekend was promised and it's what we got and more.

We got into our coach outside the Royal Pavilion in Brighton full of beans and excited for what was to come.

Our hostess on the coach was a Bette Davis as 'What ever happened to Baby Jane' lookalike in full slap and drag.

We had packed copious amounts of booze for the journey. Barry Barrington and I had done the catering for our group. Lots of smoked salmon sandwiches (crusts off Barry always emphasised crusts off) canapés and finger food. With proper napkins and plates. Barry had made coloured ice cubes in the shapes of stars and hearts out of water and different food colourings. Lemon, Lime and orange wedges. We started on Bloody Marys before progressing onto Vodka and tonics.

We thought it was taking ages to get out of Brighton because of the traffic. But no the coach we had been allocated couldn't get out of 2nd gear and it stayed that way until 8 hours later when we turned up at Butlin's in Skeggie pissed tired and emotional.

The coach driver had got lost because some of the locals had heard we were all coming and had been out and turned the street signs around directing us back out of the resort.

Unbelievable in this day and age but the Sun newspaper had got wind of it and splashed it on its front pages. "Gays and queers to invade family holiday resort Butlin's in Skegness. Local families fear they will catch Aids" That sort of thing.

The local Mayor tried to ban us from going in fear of their lives. Ignorance and homophobia was Queen then.

Butlin's tried to cancel the event but couldn't get out of the contract and so it went ahead.

It was a riot from the moment we were met off the little choo choo trains by a very large drag queen called the 'Mighty Pearl' in a dashing pink coat with a huge blonde wig, white skirt and fluffy bedroom slippers. We piled onto the trains to go to reception to check in and went to our chalets to change. Luxury it was not.

We headed back to the bar with about 2000 others it seemed. Head pink coat was Lily Savage aka Paul O'Grady who was our leader and chief bingo caller for the weekend. Aided by his dear friend Vera as Chalet maid Peggy. All the 'girls' wore Pink coats as a nod to Butlin's traditional red coats. Also on the staff was Adrella, Regina Fong, Ebony, Katherine Heartburn and various other entertainers of the day.

We did not stop laughing or partying for 3 days. The entertainment line up was terrific.

A full Orchestra lead by Mike Smith, Mike Terry (the northern Liberace and Dorothy Squires impersonator) George Logan as Dr Evadne Hinge of hinge and Brackett fame, The bay city Rollers, our very own Maisie Trollette plus many others, and top of the bill as a big surprise was the legendary Eartha Kitt. Compared by Lily Savage and Adrella the entertainment was practically nonstop for the whole event.

Paul O'grady describes the whole thing in his book "open the cage Murphy" and says they were three of the happiest days ever in his professional career.

Competitions ran from who has got the best bum competition around "the Olympic size swimming pool" To the handbag throwing competition in a nearby field.

Won incidentally by the Sun newspaper reporter they had smuggled in to report on all the depravity that was supposedly taking place.

He left disappointed I'm afraid. Although there were all night parties in all the chalets after the bar shut, these were all mainly just that. Most people were too pissed and doing the conga to have rampant sex.

I'll never forget the Butlin's safety staff hooking drag queens out of the pool with butterfly nets. Many had attempted the water slide worse for wear in full drag. Swimsuits with fishnet stockings and stilettos and wigs got a bit soggy.

The bar ran out of a week's supply of booze by 10 pm on the first night and nearly caused a riot while they closed and sent out for emergency orders until they could restock the next day when an army of draymen's Lorries arrived.

On the last day there was a huge farewell concert featuring all of the acts, except the Rollers, (not sure why they were there anyway Shang a lang hardly being a gay anthem) Adrella came out and mimed to Eartha Kitts 'Champagne taste and beer barrel pockets' number until the real Eartha Kitt stormed through the curtain pushing Adrella out of the way. The cheers at the end of the show would have done Wembley stadium proud at a cup final win. After us all singing Lily the Pink to an emotional Lily Savage, Lily led us all in 'goodbye campers see you in the morning' the finale was Mike Terry on the grand piano singing 'I am what I am' there wasn't a dry eye in the house. Nobody wanted to go home. It was without doubt the best weekend I've ever had like that. A precursor to pride really and better than any Pride I've been to also, Magic.

(Years ago I put several clips of this event on You Tube they have had thousands of hits. Type in my name and they will come up)

43

DENIS EGAN AND EILEEN WHITE

My friend that night at the London Cole Porter Aids benefit was another character. He had been a child actor and had appeared in several films as one of Will Hays (a famous comic actor in the 40's) boys, Charles Hawtrey of the carry on films was another. Later he progressed into musicals mainly in the chorus but some bigger parts to.

He moved out to Hollywood and got a few small roles, then went into the antique business helping the stars furnish their homes. Back in England he bought a hotel in Victoria, plus a famous London restaurant called "Nel Gwyns' near Baker Street (the Joe Allen of its day) where he was famous for taking the orders then disappearing into the kitchen and bringing the plates back stark naked! In the late 1980's in slightly reduced circumstances, he had ended up owning and running a pet shop in Brighton called 'Paws and claws' and doubling up by working as a barman at the Coliseum in London at night. He was always telling me stories of this woman he worked with at the Coliseum called Eileen. One weekend she was coming to stay for the weekend and he said 'oh you must come down for a drink and I'll introduce you to Eileen, you will love each other"

When we met I could not believe it. Eileen was the glamorous woman I had met years before when my pants flew into her soup at the Cafe Fleur at Spud Murphy's birthday party.

She hadn't changed a bit. I had seen her a few times at nightclubs in the west end. At the time she owned and ran the 'Marlborough head' in Drury Lane where her famous customers included Muhammad Ali and Dorothy Squires, both known for being able to put up a good fight. I'd seen her at the clubs, always sat at the bar dripping in gold and diamonds surrounded by an entourage of adoring gay men but I didn't know her.

Now she was about to become a friend for life and we are still friends now.

In London Eileen White was known as "black Eileen" or "Spanish Mary" This was because of her dark complexion. Scrapped back hair in a tight bun a'la Maria Callas she eventually became the poster girl for The Coliseum and her photograph was on bill boards and buses all over London with the caption "Not all our rounds are applause" Always chic and glamorous Eileen was a famous face in London's clubland. Originally an east end girl from Hackney a true Londoner, she has never found out where her dark almost Indian complexion came from. A DNA test suggested maybe the Spanish Amarda's invasion of Ireland.

Now she was going to become part of the Brighton family too. Having given up her long tenancy of the 'Marlboro head' in Drury Lane and a brief sojourn to a pub in Stockwell south London which she didn't like, she was working in the stalls bar at the London Coliseum opera house within walking distance of her fabulous pad just off of Shaftesbury Avenue.

44

RARE HOLIDAYS

Eileen in her spare time often came to stay and help out at the club. She was able to stay over with Colin on the rare occasion I had a holiday to help out and keep him company which was great. I did usually take the first week in January off. After weeks of cooking Christmas Lunches and Dinners and the big New Years Eve party I was ready for it.

Swales and I used to take off for Grand Canaria to the gay resort of Playa Del Ingles.

On an early morning flight to Las Palmas we got onto the plane tired and ready for a rest and some fun. We were wearing matching tie waist camel hair coats, hats and sunglasses ready to settle down have a drink and sleep.

This air hostess came up to me once people had settled down and said "excuse me sir, would you mind moving to the back of the plane?" Why I said the flights not full and I've booked this seat.

She said "well we'd like you to move as we need to re distribute the weight"

Well! I went berserk! How dare you speak to me like that! I could have slapped her. Who do you think you are talking to, I've never heard anything like it, if you need to re distribute the weight you fat cow I suggest you move your fat arse up the back yourself.

I've never been a morning person.

Well this caused quite a scene as you can imagine. The woman was nearly in tears but I was mortally offended. I wasn't fat. A bit chubby maybe but certainly not fat.

It turned out because the flight wasn't full and everyone was sitting in the front they wanted to move a few people up to the back for takeoff. However she hadn't put it to me like that.

Sitting behind us to the side were two gay men. When we got to the resort, a gay complex for gay men only. Swales and I were having a drink at the bar. We introduced ourselves to these two; their names were Gary and Mike.

After a couple of drinks and some general banter they told us "we saw you on our flight, we were sitting behind you. We heard what the stewardess said to you, we thought you were going to hit her. We said oh God I hope they are not on our bus for the transfer" then when we were, "Oh God I hope they are not staying at the same resort as we are, which we were. We had a good laugh and that was the start to an enduring friendship that has lasted for years. Gary and Mike I class as two of my dearest friends and we have had many holidays and adventures together all around the world. Gary is a few years younger than me and he's like my little brother.

Holidays were rare then. A week in the Canaries and then a week or two in Sitges in Spain in June if we were lucky.

I went with Swales usually or John Braine. Then Colin would go with Swales as well. So Swales got plenty of holidays as we had to go separately because of the club.

Later on we had many opportunities to travel further afield and we did.

45

DOROTHY SQUIRES

Denis Egan was great friends of my idol Dorothy Squires. In 1990 another good friend of mine Brian Ralphe (Vera) had persuaded Dorothy to come out of retirement and to appear at the Brighton Dome in concert.

Brian was a Brighton taxi driver turned Impresario. He had many friends in the theatre and was often out and about with Carol Kaye of the Kaye sisters, Dora Bryan and June Brown (Dot Cotton 'east enders')

I knew Carol Kaye well and her husband Len Young who I used to call Golda. Brian used to bring them to the club for lunch and they became members. We were well known for serving the best most authentic Salt Beef sandwiches in Sussex. The Jewish clientele loved them.

Lenny was a Jewish Impresario and he encouraged Brian to contact Dorothy Squires and try and get her to come out of retirement. Dot was in her late 70's then and not easily persuaded. However she was short of money and agreed. She had a soft spot for Brighton and the Dome being a reputable high end theatre encouraged her.

It was on and off for ages. Dorothy was known for being "difficult" She was a perfectionist and a professional. She only agreed if she could have a full orchestra and her musical director and saxophonist Johnnie Gray.

Eventually the great day came Saturday March 17th 1990. All day there were nervous phone calls going on back on fourth. John Nathan Turner the BBC producer and who offered Brian Ralphe lots of advice on putting this event on was sitting at my bar. They had a code going for her and eventually JNT said to me "Phew the eagle has landed". Meaning Dorothy had arrived for Band call. (Rehearsal)

She was late as she had decided en route to stop and exercise her voice in a field full of cows. Dorothy had a powerful voice and must have frightened the cattle a bit.

However ShowTime arrived and Dorothy didn't disappoint.

She did her full two hour show singing all her hits Say it With Flowers, Till, The Gypsy, I'm Walking behind you all of them. It was a very emotional experience for her and the audience.

Dorothy Squires had been a huge star in her day and had a massive gay following. She was the British/ Welsh Judy Garland. One of the biggest stars in Britain in the 1940's, 50's, 60's and 70's. As big as Shirley Bassey and Vera Lynn. This was her first live concert in many years so it caused a bit of a sensation. Although not perfect, Dot forgot a few words, she got emotional and exasperated with herself once or twice, but nobody cared she still bought the house down and got several standing ovations.

When you left a Dorothy Squires show you knew you had been to an event. She was a star and it shone through.

I had loved her since my childhood with Aunty Pat playing me Dot's hits in her flat in Primrose hill, now I was going to get the chance to meet her.

Dot stayed on in Brighton for a week or so. She had lots of friends in Brighton and was doing the rounds. I first met her the night after the show. Brian Ralphe took me with him to a private dinner party some fans were throwing in her honour in Hove and we were invited for drinks after dinner.

She was charming and on her best behaviour and we all had our photos taken with her.

Later in the week Dennis Egan phoned me and said make sure you're at the Queens arms tonight. Come down I've got a surprise for you. David Raven was appearing as Maisie Trollette and he had been on the first half of the bill at the Dome with Dorothy on Saturday night along with Mike Terry the pianist.

Anyway we turned up and of course Dennis was there with Dorothy. We spent a fun evening together watching David's act, then Colin and I went back to Denis's flat with Dot for nightcaps.

I was in seventh heaven. Colin not as star struck as me said eventually "come on get a cab it's time to go home, Dot can we give you a lift?" She was staying near us in Queens Park so she said yes. Anyway when the three of us were in the cab I said I don't want to go to bed do you want to come up for a drink Dot? Yes she said "I'm wide awake"

We had a great time just Dot and me. Colin went to bed. I got Dot something to eat and a cup of tea! She didn't want another drink. We talked all night. She made me laugh when she said "do you know that cunt Brian Ralphe? I said yes why? She said "I thought he was a top producer, turns out he's a fucking taxi driver in the day time", She tipped out her huge handbag and said "look the cunts paid me the balance in 50p pieces!" I couldn't stop laughing, at least she had got paid, and she said "I wouldn't go on without the lot upfront."

We listened to some of her recordings and I played her greatest hits on the piano while she sat on the floor at my feet singing (just quietly) along. It was a huge honour for me and a memory to cherish.

She was lovely company we talked about all sorts. I was impressed when she was telling me about her ex husband film star and James Bond Roger Moore. What had been one of the most acrimonious heartbreaking and public divorces in history had now in her mind mellowed in time and she was remembering him fondly. That may have been because of the terrific high she was still on from the Dome concert I don't know but she said we were married very happily for many years.

As Dawn came up at about 5.30am I kissed Dot Goodbye and put her in a taxi. She had signed one of the rare Dome posters for me adding on the poster "May I say, you've kept me up all night you twit but I loved it."

I never saw her again but for a few years she and I telephoned and wrote to each other regularly. She was living with two great friends of hers Des and Pete at the time. Des and Pete were regular visitors to Brighton and used to stay with Dennis Egan. Dot wanted to move to Brighton and I found her a nice flat overlooking the marina. However it wasn't to be and in hindsight maybe for the best. I wrote a song for her called "So many times" I sent her the tape and she liked it and wanted to see me to arrange it and alter it a little but it wasn't to be.

She died in 1998 of cancer of the bladder. Her last years were not happy ones. I managed to get a letter to her and her secretary Hilda Brown told me they read it to her shortly before she died and that the letter made her smile. I hope so.

I attended her funeral in Streatham in London. Dorothy had two funerals one in Wales and then the second one with the internment in London. Dorothy's Father was buried here and she wanted to be buried with him.

It was a typical funeral day gray and raining. Dorothy Entered in her coffin to "We'll keep a welcome in the hillside" and after many tributes from fellow stars, Russ Conway recreated their big hit 'Say it with flowers' on an electric piano.

I sat next to drag and music hall performer Dockyard Doris real name Colin Devereaux who was totally overcome with grief and spent most of the service with his head in my lap crying, my trousers were soaked. We said goodbye to Dorothy at the graveside where there were lavish arrangements from Shirley Bassey, Douglas Darnell and of course Roger Moore.

46

GILLIAN BURNS

On one of my many visits to the Theatre Royal Brighton with Denis Egan we were in the 'Colonnade bar' next door during the interval. He was chatting away to Victor Spinneti the Welsh actor famous for the Beatles films, who was with this gorgeous brunette. She turned around to me and with a huge white toothed smile said "Hello I'm Gilly Burns who are you". We chatted away for the short interval time and thought no more of it.

A few years went by and Brian Ralphe said to me "do you mind if I bring a friend with me to Sunday Lunch?' I moaned oh Brian do you have to? Anyway he said "I've got this girl with me she's lovely you'll love her" It was Gillian Burns.

I remembered her straight away and from that day a long and special friendship arose. In fact Gilly is one of the dearest real friends I've ever had and it's mutual.

The daughter of 50's singing star Ray Burns and cousin to Georgia Brown, the west end star of Lionel Bart's "Oliver" Gilly was a successful singer in her own right. She had taken over the role of Nancy at the Albery theatre in the West End and starred in Oliver with various "Fagin's" including Brighton based Victor Spinetti. Gilly did over 2,000 performances as Nancy in the west end and on tour and is acclaimed by her peers as being the best Nancy since Georgia Brown.

She cut various records, appeared on many TV shows here and overseas and even sang with Elvis in Las Vegas.

She was now living temporarily in the basement flat of Victor Spinetti's house in Dorset Gardens in Kemp Town while she was searching for her own place.

Victor lived there with his long term partner Graham but he was often away on tour or filming so it suited him to have Gilly living there to keep an eye on things,

Victor kept a very bohemian house and it was always full of guests. Barbara Windsor often stayed there if appearing at the Theatre Royal as did Jim Davidson and many actors who were appearing somewhere nearby. One frequent guest was the Legendary Joan Littlewood of the Stratford East theatre. So it was a colourful bunch. Once we became friends he noticed I was very tired and I had booked a week to go to the canaries for a break. "When you come back, don't go straight back to work come and stay here downstairs for a few days to recover and recharge your batteries" It was very kind of him and I took him up on his offer. He was a great and a famous raconteur and he could keep you laughing for hours at his stories.

One Sunday lunch time he turned up to the Rottingdean club for lunch and he brought Joan Littlewood with him.

He said I'm starving what's on the menu, his face fell as I explained we didn't do lunch on Sundays. However, I said don't worry go and find a seat in the garden and I'll see what I can do. I rustled them up a platter of smoked salmon sandwiches and some other nice bits and pieces, different quiches etc they were delighted. Victor said "did you have a nice time in Spain then" "Yes thanks it was great I replied" Joan attired in her usual trouser suit and communist Lenin cap bellowed, "AH the poor bloody Spanish!" I said "well there not so poor now Joan, it takes hours in the bank in the queue to withdraw money as its packed with the Spanish paying it all in" "Bloody good job after what those poor fuckers had to go through in the 1930's!" she replied.

While they tucked in I kept looking at the window above their seat. The old hotel that adjoined the club had been converted into small cottages and one of them had been bought by Michael Aspel the presenter of the TV show 'This is your life' I thought he's going to do a double take if he looks out of the window and see's these two legends he'd presented the red book to sitting right under his bedroom window.

I also got to know Gilly's parents Ray and Tilly Burns's very well as they were often down for the weekend. Ray would keep us enthralled with his stories. He was a singer with most of the big bands like Geraldo in the 40's and 50's. He'd had two huge hits both sides of the Atlantic with a song called "Mobile" and "That's how a love song was born"

His best friend for a time was Hollywood star Dana Andrews who apparently was a very badly addicted alcoholic. Dana took Ray to visit Elizabeth Taylor and Richard Burton at their suite at the Dorchester hotel and disappeared for days according to Tilly. The same thing happened when he went to one of Dorothy Squires legendary parties at her huge house St Mary's mount In Bexley Heath Kent. Ray was a bit of a naughty boy then and loved a party.

Gilly eventually moved into a flat next door to us in Queens Park Road. She had a little housewarming party with us, comedian Marty Feldman's Widow Loretta, Peter Sellers ex wife Ann, Victor Spinetti and Jean Hirigoyen. We laughed until our stomaches hurt that night. Gilly along with her parents Ray and Tilly were often my guests at Queens park road for Sunday lunch. We always had a good singsong around the piano afterwards. Ray still had a beautiful voice. Once during a doze after the lunch I put a Ray Burns record on. Thinking he was asleep Terrie Varley piped up in her broad Lancashire accent, "Oh for fucks sake, ave we got to listen to that coont singing again." Well Ray wasn't asleep and he heard her. He thought it was hilarious and often quoted the story afterwards.

Eventually the time to move came and Gilly came in from next door to help me pack. We were going through dozens of old theatre programmes when I came across one for Oliver dated around 1979. I had been to see it with John Braine and we both were very moved at the time by Nancy who I had noted in the programme had moved me to tears when singing "As long as he needs me" Now 15 years later helping me to sort through them was the Nancy we had seen. I'd not realised I had seen 'My Gilly' in it. How strange was that?

Ray sadly died in 2009 of cancer. Before he died, Gilly knowing he was seriously ill decided to arrange a big tribute night for him.

She took all his catalogue of recordings to a studio and arranged for all the 78 rpms recordings to be transferred onto CD and released the CD under the title "Tribute" It is a wonderful collection of Rays recordings with all the big bands of the era plus solo recordings. Rays style was similar to Matt Monroe and Sinatra.

For the tribute evening Gilly hired a large suite at the Cafe Royal in London, booked a great band and invited all their friends and family. As well as well known show business people there were a lot of London's Gangland faces. Ray had known the Krays well and often performed in their clubs like The Regency. I asked him once why he performed there and he replied "I'm from the East End. If in those days you got a phone call from the Krays asking you do come and sing you did it. Besides they paid well"

Well obviously the Krays were not at the party Ronnie was dead and I think Charlie was in prison as was Reggie. I never met them, but I did have the dubious "honour" of singing down the phone to Charlie Kray. His Partner Diane was a guest at one of my Sunday lunchtime Soirees and insisted I sang "Over the Rainbow to him" poor man. He was very gracious and said "you've got a lovely voice Jeremy Ronnie would have loved that"

The 'Tribute' evening was a big success. I took a party of eight friends Gary and Mike and old (Vauxhall days) friends Trevor

Rainbow and John Walker (Scottish John) plus a couple of good customers Hazel and Les, Colin and myself.

We stood in the foyer for a while, and I chuckled to myself at my guests faces as they saw people like Freddie Forman arrive and Mad Frankie Frazer with Marilyn Wisbey, Tony Lambrianou, Joey Pile and others. Show business and the gangster culture had often gone hand in hand.

I introduced my gang to the 'Godfather' Freddie Forman and his partner Janice who I had met on other occasions with Gilly and he was his usual charming self. Tony Lambrianou offered to buy us all a drink, it was a very sociable occasion.

Ray performed with the band after dinner and was incredible.

The highlight was a message from Clarence house from The Queen Mother. She wished Ray well and hoped he had a wonderful evening. This was read out by Freddie Forman's son the East ender actor Jamie Forman.

It transpired that the Queen Mothers favourite song had been the "Dark town strutter's ball" and Ray had sung it for her at Buckingham Palace.

I was honoured a few years later in April 1999 when Gilly asked me to escort her to Lionel Bart's funeral at the Golders Green Crematorium in London. Gilly was great friends with Lionel through her Cousin Georgia Brown and also for playing Nancy herself in Oliver.

Lionel had had a sad end to his life, but his funeral was a packed, star studded affair. Barbara Windsor arrived and all the paparazzi flash bulbs went off and there were lots of actors from his musicals like Toni Palmer and Miriam Karlin. Russ Abbot, Tim Rice, Donavan and Cameron Mackintosh. Peter Straker sang a very moving version of 'If you go away' at the end they played Georgia Brown singing 'As long as he needs me' very emotional. I sat next to the composer Don Black and had to remember to read the prayer book back to front as they do at Jewish Funerals.

Afterwards there was a splendid wake held at Kenwood House in Hampstead. It was in the huge kitchen. A nice sociable occasion. I made Barbara Windsor laugh when I told her I was in a borrowed suit belonging to a friend of hers Jean Hirigoyen. I'd been staying with Jean and Scott st Martyn when Gilly phoned. Jewish funerals are always quick so I didn't have time to go back to Brighton for one of my own. A tight belt and a few pins did the trick.

47

FUDGES

Every first Sunday in the month between 1983 and 2001 most of the "Glitterati" of Brighton gathered at Fudges Restaurant on Brighton seafront opposite the West Pier it was owned and run by Dick James and Malcolm Fudge and it was brilliant.

We used to often have a regular table for 12 for various guests for what were to become one of the highlights of the month.

For a set price we would have a very good value 3 course lunch (our bar bills used to be astronomical though) and a cabaret act for the afternoon. Everyone in the drag world who was any good appeared there. Phil Starr, Maisie Trollette, Scott st Martyn, Dockyard Doris, Nicky Young, Dave Lynn. Even Paul Zerdin the ventriloquist who went on to win Americas got Talent appeared there a few times. Lots of guest acts would get up and do a number Gillian Burns, Jae Alexander, Barbara Windsor even Ruby Wax!

They were great occasions and much missed. We even had my father Dons 70th surprise birthday there. We attended many theme birthday parties over the years and they were extravagant very camp and terrific fun. It is a great tribute to Dick and Malcolm that people still talk about these days with much affection.

We didn't take ourselves very seriously then, political correctness hadn't been invented and anything went. It was much better. We didn't give ourselves titles and weren't perpetually offended if someone called you a name as long as it was done affectionately. The only thing we didn't like being called was "Queer" These days gay people refer to themselves as "Queer" which I still find horrible. The idea being if you "own" the name people can't use it to insult you. Sorry guys that doesn't work for me.

48

Hi di Hi

Just before our Beau arts ball fundraising ball an old friend of mine from the curtain club days, John phoned me up one Sunday morning and said I'm down in Worthing staying with Su Pollard, she's appearing in Sweet Charity next week and is rehearsing. She's got a day off and at a bit of a loss what to do on Sunday can we come over? Yes of course I said. When they arrived Su was like a whirling dervish, she flew around our house looking in all the rooms, "ooh blimey this is bloody gorgeous this is" "Ooh Peter come and ave a look"

She was along with John accompanied by her husband Peter Keogh and old friend Ginny. Su was a very big star then, her TV hit Hi di hi playing chalet maid Peggy Ollerinshore had just ended and she was going back to her roots, musical theatre.

I took them all over to the Rottingdean club. It was a lovely sunny day and we all sat out in the garden drinking champagne and laughing. Su is the same off TV as on, outrageous and created a bit of a stir. We had a small party of Down's syndrome children in the garden and I'll never forget how kind and sweet Su was with them.

Later in the afternoon I took them off to a Brighton club where they were having a cancer fundraising day.

I got in Ginny's car with Su and Peter to show them the way and John went with Colin. On the way over a high point of the South

Downs at Woodingdean, a wasp flew in the car and went straight up the leg of Peter's shorts and stung him at the top of his leg near his groin.

By the time we got to the club he was starting to be in agony. We were at the bar and Su said what are we going to do? Peter had dived in to the toilets I said I know what's good for that and got large vodka from the barman. I passed it to Su who downed it in one. I said no you silly tart it's to rub in Peters sting, it will take the sting out. "Oh" she said got another and went off to the toilets.

A few minutes later all hell broke out, Su had been on her knees in the toilets attending to Peter's sting, he was standing up with his shorts around his ankles when a drunk with a camera barged in and took a picture. Well you can imagine what it looked like! She came running out hysterical "Oh god it's going to be all over the Sun, Su Pollard caught giving a man a blow job in a public lavy"

The drunk said I just wanted a picture of that Wollard woman; we got the camera off him and destroyed the film. Once things calmed down we had a great time and Su helped raise hundreds of pounds for this cancer charity. Which was good of her on her day off. The next week Tracy got a coach up from the Queens Arms and we all went over to see Su in Sweet Charity in Worthing she was amazing in the role. After the show we all met up in the bar. Su remembered the names of everyone she had met that day at the charity event. Impressive and lovely lady.

49

JET SETTING

Chipmunk and Robert Clarke had done very well in the nursing home business. They were very good at it and really looked after the elderly people in their care. Robert was a bit of a mentor to me in those days and I looked up to him, he was always encouraging and used to say "You'll do it one day you'll be successful, I can tell" which was nice and it did spur me on a bit.

Robert decided he would retire when he was 40 and to celebrate decided to throw a big party. In Spain.

They had bought a villa near Estepona on the Costa del Sol and invited a huge crowd over to celebrate his 40th. This was an unusual thing to do then; People didn't just hop on planes to anywhere as they do now so it was quite an event. He bought most of the tickets up on a flight to Gibraltar invited most of our Brighton crowd, his family and The Vauxhall tavern crowd.

There was much hilarity and drinking at the airport and on the flight where even the air hostesses were sporting 'Nobby's Tours' badges. (Nobby was Roberts nickname)

So when we trundled through with our luggage at Gibraltar airport we were shocked and surprised to be met by a mad man dressed in a long gown and a fez trying to sell us dirty postcards. It was David Raven Maisie Trollette in disguise. We were all in hysterics as he whipped Tracy Davenport up into his arms and run off with her trying to sell her to some men passing by. Robert had flown him out earlier to surprise us.

With all the laughing and screaming going on we soon noticed a large gathering of armed police gathering opposite to see what all the noise was. So we got onto the hired coaches and were whisked off to their villa. Robert and Chipmunk had thought of everything they had rented several villas that we all shared, there were welcome packs for everyone and the party never stopped for 4 days! It really was unforgettable. There were a few dramas of course. A few cars got written off, The Baron left a handbag full of money on a window ledge outside a restaurant, which was amazingly still there the next morning. David Raven did his party piece of hiding in wardrobes and under beds. We danced sang and drank until all hours and had a ball. (Clips on you tube)

50

"WE'RE GONNA BE MILLIONAIRES"

In the early 1990's Colin had been made redundant from the Merchant Navy. Now working for P&O ferries the climate had changed. Work schedules were altered and the hours were long. So he took the redundancy money offered and left.

What to now though was difficult he was in his mid fifties and wasn't going to walk into another job. Too active to sit about, I said you should go into some sort of business. We eventually decided to buy a Rolls Royce and do Chauffeur driven hire.

We knew lots of people who hired cars to go to the races, airport runs etc.

There were weddings of course, special occasions the scope seemed quite large. Being near to Glyndebourne Opera I thought we could tap into that market and I would provide luxury style hampers, Champagne and lavish picnics, It was a good idea and worked to a degree but we had some bad luck.

The Rolls Royce Silver Shadow was beautiful, chocolate brown with cream leather interior and cream leather wheel surrounds. It was second hand of course but reasonably low mileage. We got a proper trading licence for it and registered it with the local authority under the name Diplomat Rolls Royce hire and did everything properly, which is an expensive business. Colin bought a beautiful brown suit to match the car and went up to Saville row in London to get his chauffeurs cap made.

I worked on the advertising, which was a bit harder then. No internet of course so local papers that sort of thing and word of mouth. Yellow pages was the bible, but our timing was off as you had to wait a year to get into the next publication. A mistake on my part as it really was the go to place for looking up anything. The phone rang for a few years after we had finished with this enterprise.

My Friend John Nathan Turner was the producer of Dr Who and he had been asked to supply a celebrity to open Rottingdean village fete. To help with the Promotion of Diplomat Rolls Royce Hire. He suggested Colin go up to London and pick up Sylvester McCoy (Dr Who) and David Rapporport. (The Dwarf film star) and bring them down to open the village Fete. John wasn't daft and it killed two birds with one stone and got Dr Who and friend a return lift gratis to North London plus the publicity for us. It worked to some extent, Colin made the local front pages with Dr Who standing by the car, with the Dwarf sat on top of it and a very "merry" Sian Lloyd (a news of the world reporter) sprawled over the wing.

We did get some good bookings. Airports for special holidays. Weddings (which of course are only Saturday work in the main) Anniversaries etc plus a couple of Glyndebourne's. The races never took off as we were plunged into a national recession in 1992 caused by PM John Major and Black Wednesday. The Recession was hard and affected lots of businesses but of course luxury end ones like ours are the first to be hit.

The Rolls Royce while beautiful was unfortunately temperamental it could break down at the most inopportune moments.

I had a wedding booked at the Rottingdean Club and I sold the Rolls Royce hire as part of the package. It should have been a doddle. The Bride was getting married at the village church, was staying at the Old Place hotel next to the club and only wanted to go around the village green to arrive in a car. Well, the morning of the wedding the bloody thing broke down. Colin knew where to get underneath and bang it with a spanner to get it going, this usually worked but it didn't this time. I could see the guests getting ready for the wedding in the hotel next door, Stress levels soaring I eventually tracked down a White Rolls Royce that wasn't booked for the day and paid hundreds of pounds for them to come and take the bride 20 yards to the church! (I was cooking lunches and doing the catering for the wedding while all this was going on).

The next time we had got a very prestigious booking. This was to take the Queen Mothers Lady in waiting up to the London Palladium for the Queen Mothers 90th birthday celebrations. 'Lady B' lived in Sussex.

Colin went to pick up Lady B resplendent in evening gown, tiara and furs. On the outskirts of London the car broke down.

I got a phone call from Colin. We had one of the first car phones on the market installed for corporate clients. He said "I've Broken down" me Oh Christ where are you? "Brixton" Brixton! What do you mean you've broken down in Brixton? "I've broken down in Brixton near the tube station". Oh God this can't be happening couldn't you have broken down somewhere else? Where's Lady B? "I've put her on the tube". WHAT! Are you mad? Brixton then was very rough! You can't put the Queen Mothers Lady in waiting on the fucking tube in Brixton! "Well I have and she's gone because she doesn't want to be late"

I was mortified and shaking like a leaf and felt sick. I could just see Lady B going down the escalator in full evening dress tiara and furs surrounded by Rastafarians and drug dealers.

Anyway the end of this disaster did have a happy ending. Lady B arrived unscathed in time to look after the Queen Mother. Colin was able to do the spanner thing and got the car going again, so he was able to use the special security pass to park in Argyle street right outside of the Palladium and collect Lady B. She thought it was a huge joke and gave Colin a very big tip.

However that was the end of the line for Diplomat Rolls Royce hire. The stress wasn't worth the money. Colin sold it at auction did the local "knowledge" and bought a taxi instead.

Back in Brighton the party carried on. The 'Queens arms' was heaving as were 'Secrets' nightclub and 'Revenge' Tony Chapman's new club after he sold The Beacon Royal hotel. The town was busy and swinging. There were lots of other gay bars like the 'Bulldog' and the 'Aquarium'

People were out to have a good time they didn't spend their social time staring at their phones and I think that era between 1983 and 2000 was Brighton's finest hour.

51

THE ROTTINGDEAN CLUB (PART TWO)

My parents had been talking about retiring for some time. My mother was tired and wanted to go and live in their lovely new detached house in Saltdean with a sea view. Years of living above the shop had made her wish to live in a normal home again. At that time if you were a licensee you had to live on the premises. You couldn't lock it up and go and sleep somewhere else that was the law. It wasn't very nice because even if you made the living accommodation comfortable you could still hear people in the bar downstairs or someone would shout up the stairs to ask where something was.

Colin and I had been looking around for about a year for a pub of our own in Brighton. Colin had given up the taxi (too stressful) and had been working behind the bar in the club for a while now. We couldn't find anywhere suitable. Most of them were hovels that needed lots of money spent on them. The Breweries never liked spending any money on their own buildings they expected the tenants to do that. It was a bloody cheek, You were tied to sell their beer, paid rent and had a full repairing lease where you were liable for everything in the building, roofs, damp, electrics, equipment everything. They got greedier and greedier as the years went on and made some publicans pay them a percentage of their food takings and fruit machines as well.

One day it just came to me. We had been looking at all these grotty places when we were already in one of the best bars in the area. I said to mum, why don't Colin and I buy you and dad out so you can retire. She didn't flinch and said yes.

Of course it was the obvious answer we had all been there for 10 years, I'd been doing the catering for 8 years the business was established and good.

My dad didn't really want to retire he hated change but he was 67 by then and mum 65 so it was time.

It was all done properly. I insisted that they got the business valued by a broker and that we paid them what it was worth, the market value. We couldn't afford to pay them in one lump so it was arranged to pay so much a month until the amount was paid off. I'm pleased to say that we did so well we were able to pay them back the full amount plus 5% interest on top within 2 years.

This arrangement worked well, because it meant my dad could keep his hand in and did our nights off for us. Which meant he could see his friends and have a drink and a laugh as well. My mother still provided me with pounds of fresh pastry several times a week and helped out when we had party nights and functions which was often. We had always worked well as a family, we never fell out and argued as some families do. This Worked, because we all had our own designated jobs or our own departments to run.

We probably had a few arguments but not many. So everyone was happy. Mum and dad were also at last able to enjoy some lovely holidays and went off on several well earned luxury cruises and coach tours all over Europe.

The downside for Colin and I and the big sacrifice was having to move out of our beautiful home in Brighton and move above the Rottingdean Club. The accommodation was limited. Two bedrooms and an attic office/guest room sitting room kitchen and bathroom. Because of the age of the building there was lots of low beams to bang your head on, the floors sloped a bit and were on different levels. I hated it. There was no central heating and it was bitterly cold in the winter. I used to put more clothes on to go to bed than when I got up.

I got the whole place re carpeted and decorated and did make it into a fairly nice home. We didn't want to spend a fortune on heating as my parents had done that at the 'Talbot' as it was dead money improving the breweries property.

So with my father and I dressed in our best suits and ties we went to court to get my licence and in 1994 aged 34 I became the Landlord of the Rottingdean Club.

The customers presented my parents with a nice farewell plaque and we had a goodbye party for them.

Then we had our reopening night with Colin and I as the new landlord's. Lots of people came to wish us well but one person touched me very much by her kindness.

My old friend Winnie Sexton from the Cricketers in Brighton came over in a taxi to wish us well. She stayed for several hours. She must have been in her 70's then! She had a handbag full of cash and bought everybody a drink as they came in the door. (This was the traditional way we in the licensed trade used to ensure that fellow publicans had a good first days takings) although Winnie was exceptionally generous that day. She left in the same taxi with its meter still running after wishing us all the best and giving us some very good advice. Pure class.

My parents were old school publicans and my father always wore a shirt, tie and jacket behind the bar. My mother always had smart dresses too. In the early years at the 'Talbot' they used to wear full evening dress Friday and Saturday nights behind the bar. Seems over the top now but it used to be said, "You should dress the same as the type of customers you wish to attract". This definitely made a difference then.

When we took over we carried on the tradition. Colin always wore a shirt and tie and I always wore a smart jacket and trousers. Never jeans and our staff were not allowed to either.

We encouraged our customers to be the same and we didn't allow people in the bar in shorts and T shirts, whatever the weather. However the atmosphere was far from stuffy.

Although I had worked at the club for 8-10 years and Colin and I knew everyone, there was still a bit of animosity to us about taking over.

There was definitely some homophobia. Rumours were rife, we were going to turn it into a gay club. When I realised which group had said it, loudly one night within their earshot I said, "Stupid isn't it I've heard we are going to make this place into a gay club. There are dozens of gay bars in Brighton so why the hell would people want to schlep all the way out here and mix with some of this lot" Likewise when I heard the "you'll have to keep your backs to the wall now lads comments" I'd reply "no need, you'd have to be good looking or at least half decent for that to happen. You've got no problem with a face like that".

That's the way you deal with that sort of thing. Pick the ring leader and make them look an idiot. These days they'd be arrested for a hate crime and everyone would have to go for counselling.

We did have quite a lot of gay customers anyway, my mother always liked the gay boys and made lots members before we took over. Lots of the Brighton crowd and entertainers used to come over for lunch. One day Dockyard Doris (a larger than life character in all ways) was sitting in the garden with Maisie Trollette and entourage, I went out to see if everything was alright when I noticed Doris had a few tears running down his face. I said oh dear whatever's wrong? Grabbing my hand he said dramatically, "nothing darling, it's just that is without doubt the best ham egg and chips I've ever eaten!" (Fond of his food was Doris)

Any changes we wanted to make came up against fierce opposition at first. I decided that I wanted to do evening dinners, there was the usual moaning about the smell of food, we don't want that here etc. You just have to take no notice and do what you think is right. We did lose one or two members but we gained many many more.

I turned one end of the bar into a dining area and kept the rest food free for the drinkers.

I put together a good up to date modern menu with classical favourites on it as well for Wednesday to Friday nights. On Saturday nights I'd do a special menu and we would cloth all the tables up with the best starched linen silverware and candlelight. I bought a baby grand piano and introduced regular pianists. I had the piano miked up to the restaurant area so people could listen to cocktail jazz music during dinner. This proved to be a big hit and was usually booked out well ahead.

I trained one of the kitchen staff up to be able to cope with it, I prepared most things and taught them how to serve it so I could stay front of house and mix with the customers. Colin ran the bar and I served and did the bills with a waiter serving the food. I was still doing all the lunches so it was a nice change for me to get out front suited and booted and mixing.

It proved a big hit but after a couple of years the Wednesday and Thursday nights started to drop off. The pub over the road had become a managed house and they started doing these sizzling steaks for £6 with all the trimmings and they were very popular.

I couldn't compete on the price with steak, so I decided to do alongside our regular menu, a "Midweek Roast", this would be either Beef or Pork served with 4 fresh vegetables roast potatoes and Yorkshire pudding for £5.00. I included a pudding of the day as well for that. Usually old favourites like 'spotted dick' and custard.

It was cheap even then but I made a profit. Plus not everyone had it and they would add a starter plus a bottle of wine, drinks before dinner etc. It was a big draw and within no time we were turning people away on Wednesday and Thursdays and the takings soared.

The musical evenings were successful, even those who'd moaned the most enjoyed it. Ray and Tilly Burns were often down and Gilly and Ray would get up and do a few numbers which brought the house down. Our members were mostly an older crowd and many remembered Ray from their youth and couldn't believe they were hearing him in Rottingdean. I would also play and sing and Ray Tilly, Gilly and Colin had some lovely nights after we had closed (lock ins) and had jam sessions with a few close friends to wind down after work.

Another thing we gave up on taking over the business was our social life. Running a pub/ club restaurant is all time consuming. Our regular nights out and parties came to a halt. We had Monday nights off and that was it. The Rottingdean club was like a country pub so we had the same opening hours as all the pubs in the village, 7 days a week.

The difference with the club was you had to be a paid up member to come in.

This was an advantage because you could refuse any undesirables that tried to get served by saying I'm sorry we are strictly members only. On the other hand you could lose out on passing trade especially in the summer when Rottingdean has a lot of tourists. However I preferred it. We were very strict on who became a member and if I didn't like the look of someone they wouldn't get in. It wasn't based on class or money it was just a gut instinct. I let a few horrors through in my time as well, not rough, but difficult types, the worst being some of the "ladies who lunch".

It had its snob appeal too, people love to say "oh do come to my club for lunch or dinner" especially business people trying to impress a client. It was an unusual set up but the membership money helped pay the rent on the building to.

The only time we closed for the day was on the day of Princess Diana's funeral. I like other people was shocked and very upset at Diana's death. I wanted to watch the funeral in private, in peace. It was not the sort of occasion you could put a TV in the bar and watch it with a pint in your hand like a football match, so we closed for the morning and afternoon out of respect.

We had some very good regular drinkers. People then really did booze. One couple used to come in every lunchtime and every night

7 days a week. 'John' used to drink 1.5 litres of Bells whiskey every day and his wife 1.5 litres of Vodka. 'Joan' was an occasional jobbing actress (extra) and when she'd had a few could turn quite nasty. I barred her a couple of times but she'd beg forgiveness and I'd let her back in. They did spend a lot of money. She was a snob like Hyacinth Bouquet and looked and sounded like her, just drunk. One night they made their way home and cutting through the churchyard Joan passed out and slept all night on top of someone's grave. The next day a bit bedraggled she came in for a livener and was very pleased nobody had stolen her handbag. These two could be the bain of our lives sometimes, but it goes with the territory. I'll be honest and say if it wasn't for the amount they spent I would have had them out.

Plus we had lots of lovely regulars too and we just tried to ignore the awkward ones as best you could. Always serving with a smile through gritted teeth! (Teeth and tits as they say in showbiz)

After everyone got used to our way of running the club it settled down and we became very successful.

We had lots of parties. From the age of 14 I had worked every Christmas and New Year's Eve for my parents either behind the bar or DJ'ing playing all the music, now it was their turn to work for me. I liked Dj'ing and was good at gauging the mood to get everyone up dancing. It's a lonely job like playing the piano. You're entertaining while everyone around you is partying. A pianist told me once "you know when you're going down well if people only notice when you stop"! Very true that.

We used the garden to its full advantage and we had lots of big bbq's. Two of my favourite ones were when I hired a line dancing teacher and I had 100 people in the garden all learning how to line dance. Another was a Caribbean night where we went to town in the garden with the lighting and decorations and I hired a steel band for the entertainment. Great fun. No frozen burgers and cheap sausages at our bbqs it was 8oz sirloins and a marquis full of salads and desserts. They were ticket affairs for members only and always sold out.

We still did weddings, funerals, anniversaries you name it we did it. I never said no to earning money.

Most of the time we had a great staff. Some like our barmaids Sally Eisnor and Helen Horsham (Helen well into her 80's) stayed with us for the duration and were wonderfully loyal.

Others came and went and some got too big for their boots and had to go. I hope we were always good to our staff. We tried to be generous in lots of ways and always helped out if someone was in trouble if we could. Some appreciated it others thought it was their entitlement. Some are honest, some are born fiddlers. Staff are usually the number one headache when you are running a business. Small business like ours while maybe only offering part time work can help with the unemployment figures. We employed 14 people a week at various times.

52

CARY GRANTS GHOST

One of our customers was the old comedy actor Hugh Lloyd he used to be with Terry Scott and Peggy Mount in the old 1960's TV comedies like Hugh and I. Him and his wife Sian were regulars. Sian had been a top Fleet Street journalist in her time. She wanted to write a story on the club. I wasn't so keen but she talked me into it. So I gave her an interview about the building and the history of the club.

She asked if it was haunted and I told her that I had seen the ghost of this man in the middle bar. He had black shoulder length hair and wore a knee length black frock coat. He was good looking about 35 with piercing blue eyes. I'd seen him one night as I was cleaning up. (Wishful thinking everybody said) but it wasn't I saw him. He walked behind the bar smiled brushed past me and disappeared. It didn't frighten me at all. Other people over the years had spotted him to.

She went on to ask what celebrities used the club. Here I had to be discreet but I did mention that years before the club had been part of the hotel next door and one of the regular guests was the film star Cary Grant. This was true and he always had the same room, number 11 which was now one of the bedrooms we had above the club.

Bette Davis had also stayed in the village when she was on the run from Warner Brothers. Rottingdean attracted all sorts of people, Rudyard Kipling had lived there too. We talked of various other things, Sian made some notes and that was that.

Thinking no more of it about a week later she turned up with a photographer. She said "I think the local paper is interested, do you mind if we just have a few pictures"? My mum and dad were there and they got us to sit near the fireplace for some photos. Sian said can you look at this all of you? And she thrust a picture of Cary Grant into my hand. What's this for? "Oh nothing just thought I'd mention that Cary used to stay here that's all."

Well one week Later it was the front page of the local newspaper "Cary Grant's Ghost lives in the Rottingdean club" and there was the picture of me, mum and dad all staring at his photograph. I could have died.

I got on the phone to Sian furious, I said what have you done Sian? She pleaded ignorance and said that the paper had misinterpreted her copy and made a mistake. Likely story I said, "Honestly Jeremy" Sian said "but it's quite a scoop darling isn't it anyway don't worry it's only the local rag it will be forgotten in a week"

Well it wasn't forgotten in a week. Every single paper in the country got wind of it and it appeared in all of them in some form or another. In fact the story went around the world to America and even New Zealand and Australia. It was on news shows, in magazines everything.

It got quite nasty, the phone rang off the hook with reporters asking to speak to me. I kept trying to explain that it was a mistake and tell them what I had really said. But nobody was interested in the truth, they just wanted the story. One tabloid said to me, "if you're trying to hide anything Jeremy you might as well tell us now as we will find out and print it" I said there's nothing to find out which there wasn't. I even got some hate mail through the post.

The worst part was that Cary Grant's family lived nearby in Peacehaven that's probably why he used to stay there, and obviously heard about it and turned up in the bar to speak to me. It was my day off so luckily missed that and Colin explained what had happened. That we were not after publicity as we were a private club and couldn't benefit from this at all. Which was true. This story stayed on the internet for years. I hope Sian Lloyd got well paid for it but I never got a penny. It just shows you the power of the press and it also confirmed to me not to believe everything you read in the papers.

53

WE'LL MEET AGAIN

Rottingdean, was a very patriotic village and St Georges day was a big thing, a whole weekend of parties closest to April 23rd with lots of bunting and red and white flags all around the village. We used to be packed out every year with people in their red and white outfits. Plenty of union flags flying as well. We always ended up with the "last night of the proms" on the stereo with me conducting my "promenaders" standing on top of a table singing Land of hope and Glory, Rule Britannia and Jerusalem.

Twice we had big parties to celebrate the anniversaries of VE day. We had stage sets built to make the outside of the club look like a NAFI shelter (navy, army and air force institutes) with sand bags piled up outside. Eileen dressed as a wren would serve bangers n mash for everyone from the "NAFI Canteen" then when plenty of drink had been taken I would get on the piano for a big sing song. People used to really get really involved wearing original uniforms in some cases.

I've always been very patriotic and a few years before John Braine's partner my old friend Tony Finn had got us tickets for the last night of the proms. It was a fantastic occasion. I had such a lump in my throat I couldn't sing Land of hope and glory properly. Tears running down my face I looked up to see Princess Margaret with her 'toy boy' Roddy Llewellyn throwing toilet rolls out of the Royal box. She had obviously had a few. Later she walked past us on the stairs. She was incredibly beautiful with the most amazing violet coloured eyes.

I saw her years later in Le Caprice restaurant in Mayfair with Eileen and John Braine (now known to everybody as Joanie, (only because we had so many Johns in our crowd) It was shortly after Princess Diana's death so she was wearing full black. She was opposite with two friends. As she was leaving she stopped to speak to this famous actress on our right, then as she passed we rose and Eileen and I dipped our heads and she nodded, obviously very impressed with the elaborate curtsey Joanie (John Braine) had managed to drunkenly execute. She swept past George Michael on our left without as much as a glance. I was wetting myself laughing; I said to Joanie what did you do that for? He replied in broad Cockney. "I couldn't "elp meself it just came naturally"

One year the village fete committee had managed to persuade Dame Vera Lynn to come and do the official opening. She lived nearby in Ditchling. The committee picked The Rottingdean Club as the place to entertain her in afterwards.

To say I was over the moon about this is an understatement. From a little boy sitting with my grandparents listening to their 78rpm records of Vera Lynn singing Well meet again etc to the present day I was and am a massive fan. Dame Vera has a beautiful voice, perfect diction too. She was also much loved by the British public and especially ex servicemen. A true English legend and national treasure. My friend Ray Burns had known her and said "You never heard a bad word about Vera Lynn in the Business, everyone liked her."

To me this was like getting a visit from the Queen Mother. I stayed up all night the night before the big day. Baking steak and kidney pies and puddings. Lots of English things I thought she might like. On the day I wouldn't let anyone order before she came in in case I sold out of anything. So when she did arrive and order I had a massive backlash of orders on the board all at once, we were packed to the gunnels inside and in the garden too.

After all that cooking she said she was vegetarian! I could have wept! She ate fish though so was Pescatarian and had the grilled Plaice.

I had to laugh though because she had all these old RAF types running around in rings and very nervous. One old spitfire pilot said to me looking very flushed and nervous. "She's a very forth-right woman, she's told me she doesn't sign autographs and she doesn't like shaking hands" She was quite regal to look at.

After I finished serving the lunches I went out into the bar to meet her. I sat with her for ages and she was lovely, really down to earth. She still had a cockney twang, after all she was from the east end of London originally. I said do you remember a singer called Ray Burns he sometimes sings in here. She said straight away "Ray Burns of course I remember him, lovely voice, how's his wife Tilly?" Now I was impressed with that because it must have been 40+ years since they had seen each other.

When she was ready to go she stopped first to have photographs taken with whoever wanted them and I introduced her to some of the regulars and yes she shook hands to.

I'd keyed up we'll meet again to come on the CD player but it wouldn't bloody work! so we had to make do with 'I'll be seeing you' I had speakers out of the window and the whole club turned out into the street and sang and waved to her goodbye. Another lovely memory.

Colin with Dr Who Sylvester Mcoy David and Sian Lloyd

Dame Vera Lynn and me

Dorothy Squires and me

Gilly Burns Entertaining Rottingdean Club

John Terrie, me, Su Pollard, Peter Keough and Colin Rottingdean club

Landlords of the Rottingdean club

Line dancing on the Terrace Rottingdean Club.

One of many parties at club

Mum dad me dressed
up going to work

Phanotm of the opera mask ball 2

Our Rolls Royce

Ray Tilly and Gilly Burns

With Su Pollard garden Rottingdean Club

54

MORE TEA VICAR?

I was good friends with the local Vicar Father Martin Morgan, a controversial figure when he arrived in Rottingdean. He had in a previous life been a gag writer for Frankie Howard and other comedians. He was very funny.

Being a landlord then meant I had to go to lots of funerals. If a good customer died it was a sign of respect to attend the service. One day I was standing outside the church entrance waiting for the coffin to pass by when I stepped back, I felt a stab in the back of my leg and jumped a bit. I'd stepped back into a rose bush. Father Martin standing next to me and quick off the draw as ever said in a side mouth to me "I bet that's not the first time you've had a prick up your arse is it dear"! Well I burst out laughing just as the deceased passed by and got some funny looks from the pall bearers. (Father Martin was camp but not gay)

Another time Father Martin had invited us up to the vicarage for a summer party. Colin and I went with some friends of ours Brenda and Ged. Thinking oh god this is going to be a right bore, we couldn't have been more wrong. The tea party was in full swing. The "Tea" was being served by transvestite waitresses in fish net stockings and short skirts. There was dancing going on and I looked further down the garden to see a stark naked local Liberal councillor dancing around the maypole.

Father Martin said to us sorry I've got to go, I've got to take Elvie to France for a book signing. There's loads of booze under the sink in the kitchen help yourselves. He was right, there were more bottles under the sink than in the local off Licence. Elvie Rhodes was a local author who was one of our regulars at the Rottingdean club, she had lost her husband and late in life became a bestselling author. She turned to Father Martin to help her cope with her grief. He was good to her and now when he had a holiday coming up he would be her travelling companion while she went on research trips for her stories.

Father Martin did a great job in Rottingdean. He brought a community together. He introduced lots of fun to. He has his serious side, but proved you don't have to be stuffy or dour or even worse the happy clappy type to get your message across.

55

BACK ON THE LADDER

I had been thinking for some time I must start looking out for another property to buy as we will need somewhere to live when we come out of the club.

We had managed to buy the flat in London and we had Queens Park Road in Brighton. I'd let the London flat to a series of dubious tenants, the best of whom were three black prostitutes who left the flat in immaculate condition. The only ones who did.

Queens Park road we had let out to school teachers who left the place a mess.

We sold the London flat but not at the best time however, we made a reasonable profit and were glad to see the back of it.

Queens Park road also had to go which broke my heart but at the time we couldn't afford the mortgage plus the rent on the club and paying back mum and dad the loan.

This was also during a property dip but again made a decent profit. I'd invested the profits but now realised it was time to buy another home as the market was on the up and if we didn't get our foot back on the ladder we would be homeless.

I found a lovely flat on the seafront in Kemp town in Brighton. It was in one of the beautiful regency buildings, first floor with a large balcony overlooking the sea.

Colin wasn't too keen, everyone thought it was a lot of money for what it was. A two bedroomed flat. But I knew that seafront property was always an investment and only went one way, up! I was right it was one of the best investments I have ever made.

Marine Parade was a trophy flat. High ceilings, stunning sea views, central location, perfect. Its only downside was it had a tiny kitchen, but it still housed a washer dryer and a small dishwasher.

We had it redecorated and it looked stunning. I turned one of the bedrooms into a formal dining room and bought appropriate antiques to furnish it with. The drawing room overlooking the sea was beautiful.

This was going to be our bolt hole away from the pokey accommodation above the club. Somewhere to have some privacy which it was for a few years. I relished having a proper home again and it wasn't long before I was throwing dinner parties on our night off. (I know mad, but it was nice going back to a normal life style)

Now we were established, I managed to spend Sunday night and all day Monday there. Tuesday was always cash and carry stock shopping whatever the weather and we had Tuesday night there to. Colin would sleep at the club then I would come home and he would go over and sleep there. Never at the same time because one of us always had to be on call at the club.

Holiday's were the same. In 7 years we had two, 1 week holidays together. The two times we went, our usually very reliable barman got a bit power mad and went off the rails. I accepted his apology and hoped it was a one off. The second time we came home to find my Father had sacked him for being drunk on duty and inviting family and friends in for drinks on the house, as if it was his own money he was spending. So after that it had to be separate holidays. Not a bad thing if you work together as well but really upsetting when you've had your trust broken by what you thought were loyal employees.

Similarly I had employed a chef to do the evening cooking and my days off so I could be a bit more front of house, instead of being in the background sweating over a hot stove all the time.

A 22 stone transvestite. I employed him because he was a good cook and it was very hard to get good staff outside of Brighton. Plus our catering kitchen was so small nobody wanted to work in it for long.

The first day he arrived to work, having shaved his eyebrows off for a drag ball he had attended the night before. Some of the customers started snickering. I said don't be so cruel the poor man has alopecia, which shut them up.

He also felt it was his "right" to steal bottles of Gin from us and food from the freezer so he could entertain his own friends at home in a lavish manner. I couldn't prove anything but when he wanted a pay rise I said no and he gave me 2 weeks' notice. He was very shocked when I accepted straight away. I was glad to see the back of him. He was a nasty piece of work and I had had complaints from parents of some of the younger staff members about his inappropriate language and manner.

So back in the kitchen I went and I stayed doing all of the food for the next couple of years. After I had finished in the kitchen I would rush upstairs to get changed into a smart outfit to come down and spend the last hour with our customers. Even at a late hour or nearly closing time I would do this. I would never sit in the bar in my Chefs clothes.

Sunday mornings I did all the bookkeeping made the wages up and checked all the restaurant bills. Wrote cheques where needed, paid the bills, organised the banking and handled membership enquires and reminders of payment. We didn't do food Sundays because of the short licensing hours then, so it was a good time to do the office work. I still managed to get down into the bar for the last hour to have a chat with the regulars.

I was lucky that Eileen White had retired and was able to spend long spells with us helping behind the bar, waitressing, even washing up. With her experience she fitted in well at the club and was a great help. It also helped her at a difficult time when she lost her partner Jimmy suddenly.

Jimmy had been a theatre technician. Putting in the stage sets and lighting. A profession made up of mainly London Cockneys and their sons. When Jim died there were wreaths all the way around the block from where they lived from outside the flat in Grape St past the Shaftesbury theatre in Shaftesbury Avenue and right back around to the door, an amazing sight.

As soon as we closed Colin and I would take off to Brighton for something to eat. Usually a restaurant like Prompt Corner in Montpellier road, or the fabulous Aberdeen steak house in Preston Street run by Nick the Greek. I had been going there since I was 14 years old with mum and dad. Both restaurants were popular with publicans because they served late into the afternoon. To get around the archaic licensing laws in the 1970's I remember the Aberdeen steak house serving gin and vodka out of teapots, and people drinking gin and tonics out of teacups.

Once when we had finished our meal at the Aberdeen, we got a phone call to say we had been burgled at the club. It had happened before. This was just before Christmas when we had been packed for weeks doing Christmas lunches and dinners.

They broke into the safe and got all the Christmas takings and the staff tips I had got ready to bank on the Monday morning. That was a real kick in the teeth. I covered all the staff tips and the insurance covered some of our loss but it was a real blow, we've always thought it was an inside job!

56

THE MILLENNIUM

As the millennium approached I was trying to come up with a way to celebrate the year 2000 in style.

Numbers had to be limited. Normally New Years Eve we wouldn't make a door charge and we gave trays of food out to everyone for free.

This year I thought I'm going to have to restrict it because with nearly 2000 members on paper if even 300 turn up it will be too many.

So I thought right I'll do it in style I was going to charge £100 a ticket for 100 members. Champagne on arrival plus again at midnight and all other drinks fully included. Cabaret and disco plus a marquis full of delicious food.

However this did not suit some of the locals. Some of my customers were known to like a freebie and objected having to pay anything considering they coughed up their £20 a year membership fee.

I didn't want that type anyway but it caused friction. One couple who were regulars and we classed as 'semi friends' actually reported us to the police for potential overcrowding and fire risk.

Even though our license wasn't the type where there was a limit on numbers, they didn't know that and just wanted to spoil everyone else's fun because they didn't want to pay.

I got called into the police station in Brighton for an interview at a time when I could have really done without it as I was so busy with Christmas parties. These police treated me a bit like a criminal. I was very upset and offended because my family had always held spotlessly clean licences didn't break the law and took our role seriously. They couldn't do anything to stop me having my New Years Eve Ball but they said they would have someone watching me.

What they didn't know was that some of the more senior police in the area were members of the club and were coming to the party. They were also able to find out for me who had reported us.

I was shocked when I found out but I couldn't let on as I had been sworn to secrecy.

So I decided to scale down the whole affair and charged £10 each for the tickets to restrict the numbers, but only included a buffet and entertainment in the price. It was still a lovely party. The two that had reported me were not able to buy tickets as I had "Sold out"

They begged me to come as they were regulars but I said no, I'm sorry some rotten swine reported me to the police for numbers allowed so I have to be very strict on who comes in that night. Justice done!

This was really the last straw for me. After 17 years of us all giving 100%to the club, all the parties the lunches dinners and functions I had had enough.

Also for years I had suffered really bad back problems. From the early days at the club my back would go out and into spasm. Sometimes I had to do the lunches perched on a bar stool. My dad and Colin used to take me over to an osteopath in Hove three times a week to get treatment. This carried on off and on throughout my time at the club and indeed to this day. I was spending £75-100 pw on treatments just to be able to function.

So I decided to sell up. Now do you remember that I said at the beginning of the book how I got sweet justice back on the brewery for giving the pub in Brighton to somebody else? Well this is what happened.

Watney's had ceased trading and sold the freehold of the club in an asset stripping sale to Nomura Japanese bank.

So here I was a country landlord paying my rent not to a brewery but a bloody Japanese bank!

The same people ran the show though, the area managers that had worked for Watney's just transferred company logos but carried on. I tried to buy the freehold of the club but was not successful. One day they sent these little Japanese business men down to see the club to inspect the premises. It was a beautiful warm day, the garden was packed full of people. The Club had bits of land attached to it so it was a valuable site. Rottingdean has some of the prime real estate in the area. It is a wealthy village and its proximity to Brighton made it more so.

As a sitting tenant I was able to apply to buy it for a discount.

Several years before I had convinced my father to buy a "free of tie" long lease on the club for a small amount of money. This released us from the beer tie from the brewery meaning we were able to get much better deals from competing breweries. Instead of a reoccurring three year lease we now had a 20 year reoccurring lease. Which was now mine to sell.

The freehold value of the building was big. So I figured if I could buy it with a big discount I could make a nice profit.

However when they saw it the Japanese decided to keep it. I realised they had sensed that there was development possibilities.

To get a valuation on the club was quite difficult. It was a bit of an unknown quantity. Basically a pub but you had to be a member to come in. It couldn't be valued on its barrelage like they did other pubs because it was a different type of business.

So having an inkling something was in the air. I decided to bypass local pub/restaurant estate agents and called in Christie's from London to value it. Local agents were in the pockets of the local area managers and often got drunk together at pub changeover days, I knew this from experience.

The guy from Christies said well really you can ask what you like for this as it is a niche market. So I did I put it on the market with them for a high price but told them to sit on it until I was ready. This paid off.

About 6 weeks later the man from Watney's or Nomura as it was now approached me. He said "I've got some marvellous news for you. The company want to buy the club from you and are willing to offer you xxx for the lease" It was about one third of what I had put it on the market for.

I said no that's not enough I want xxxxx. "Impossible you must be joking he said, this is a good offer you should take it. The only way you can get more is if you have already marketed it for a higher price" When I put the paperwork down in front of him from Christies the colour drained from his face.

He was Flabbergasted. I loved it, he thought he could walk in and I would jump. It was the same guy who had let me down over the Brighton pub 16 years before. Nomura refused to pay me the money, he lost his commission and his face, but they couldn't get me out as I was a sitting tenant with a long lease. So I sat it out for a bit before instructing Christies to put it on the market.

In July I had my 40th birthday coming up. I decided to have a big party to celebrate but also as my swan song. We knew we were getting ready to leave but we kept it quiet.

57

40 YEARS ON

On July 6th 2000 I would be 40 years old. I wanted to have a big party but not in the Club. This time it was for me, with someone else doing the catering and the entertainment. I wanted it to be strictly invitation only, so I didn't feel obliged to invite all of my customers but just the ones who I liked and was close to. I was still a bit raw from the millennium.

Thinking about somewhere in Brighton for the event. I ran this past my dear friend Jean Hirigoyen one day.

"Non non non Jeremy you 'ave to "ave a beeg party in London darling, you are from London so it must be London" Jean is French if you haven't gathered. He also had a top job with one of the biggest hotel chains in the country.

He got on the case and arranged for me to hold my 40th at the Selfridge Hotel in Oxford Street in London. Right next to the famous store where my mother had taken me to get my haircut as a little boy and where we would go up to at Christmas to look in wonderment at their Christmas windows. So it was a very appropriate venue. He also arranged a discount price on rooms for my guests if they wanted to stay over.

I went up to London to plan it all with their events manager and head chef they were really helpful. They all adored Jean and as our old friend Barry Barrington always said "I was treated like royalty"

I booked a large Coach for all the Brighton and Rottingdean crew to wait outside Fudges restaurant in Brighton to give everyone who was coming a lift up to London and back.

I booked a great Jazz band that played for us at the club and a disco which was only allowed to play music from the 60's 70's and 80's made up of a lot of old reggae and Tamla Motown hits from my youth.

Friends and family made their own way from all over the country and many stayed overnight at the hotel.

I wanted something a bit different to wear other than a conventional suit. So I went to an Indian Shop and bought a silk cream Indian wedding suit with shoes to match. It was quite plain but very elegant. The balloon type trousers you wear under the long coat meant there was plenty of room to move about in.

Colin bought a beautiful Italian silk suit and some good suede shoes. We looked very smart even if I say so myself.

On the day Colin and I arrived and were shown to a lovely suite. I went down to check all the rooms. Gilly Burns was there before me to go through the rooms and make sure everything was just right. She's very good at organising like me so I trusted her.

Everything was in order so I went up to rest and change.

It was a superb party.

Colin and I greeted the guests at the entrance to a large reception room where very smart waiters served Champagne and canapés to all our guests.

Brian O'Connor my brother in law and photographer was poised by the door to take everybody's photograph as they arrived. Everyone was dressed up to the nines and looked fantastic.

Friends old and new came, including the Priors from Primrose hill (our old family friends) in fact they came to all our parties at the Talbot and the Club, and we are still dear friends now.

The Baron turned up in his opera cloak sporting a Burberry ensemble and a huge diamond broach. Nearly everyone I wanted to be there was.

After about an hour's reception and god knows how many bottles of champagne all the guests had arrived and I walked to the other end of the room as two doorman held back two enormous doors that led into the ballroom.

As I led the guests into the room the band struck up Over the Rainbow my favourite song. It was quite emotional. A brigade of chefs were lined up behind all the various serving tables in their full uniforms serving every type of cold meat and salad and seafood you can imagine. Huge ribs of beef in aspic, roasted hams, dressed salmons, all beautifully arranged.

I had also arranged for a full bar to go into the room and my guests could have what they wanted all night as well as plenty of wines on the tables.

The Jazz band played throughout the meal. Unplanned, Gilly and Ray got up and did a set with the band which brought the house down and I was very touched that Ray had re written the lyrics to a song we both loved to make the words a special tribute to me.

The 1960's disco went down a storm and I was presented with my birthday cake by my very young nephew and niece Jonothon and Sophie O'Connor.

It was a party I'll never forget, in some ways it was more like a wedding, but I'm unlikely to ever get married even though it is now legal, so that will do as my reception.

The only sad note was that the Baron who I briefly spoke to after the party said he had slept the night on a park bench in Hyde Park. Too drunk to get home to Clapham. None of us ever heard from him or saw him again.

Robert and Chipmunk tried via the Salvation Army to trace him, but nothing came up. He just disappeared into the ether. A much loved figure in all of our lives.

So when I was ready I quietly put the club onto the market. Within in a few weeks a nosy member had found it for sale on a website and told the whole village. You always try to keep things quiet as it disrupts your business and upsets your staff. Anyway it was out now. It wasn't easy to sell the club I had so many time wasters it was unbelievable. The sale fell through several times. Not because of the business but through people not being able to raise the finances or usually people with lack of experience who lost their nerve at the last moment.

Anyway, the time came and it did sell for nearly the asking price.

It was so sad to leave. We had letters from so many people wishing us well and thanking us for years of service. The customers clubbed together and bought us travel vouchers so we could have a proper holiday together, There were many goodbye parties and lots of tears. It was sad to leave. It had been our family home for 17 years. My niece Sophie and nephew Jonothan spent every Christmas from babies there. We would set up tables around the log fire when we closed on Boxing Day and have our family Christmas lunch there. So it was much more than just a business to us.

However when the time came, Colin and I were able to leave with our heads held high and move into our lovely flat on Marine Parade to have a nice long break and consider what to do next. I was 40 years old and had decided to retire.

58

"RETIREMENT"

The First thing I did was pay off the mortgage on the flat on Marine Parade. People advised me not to do that and to keep it for tax reasons etc. But I hate debt so I paid it off and I was right to. The roof over our heads was paid for and nobody could take it away.

Once all the taxes and bills had been paid I just about had enough to plan for the future. However we were exhausted so we rented an apartment in Sitges on the Costa Dorada in Spain for 1 month.

For the last two weeks mum and dad came out for a holiday staying in a nearby hotel. This was unbelievable to us because mum had always refused to fly. She has a terrible phobia about planes and a fear of flying caused we think through being in London in the war. Anyway she did it and we picked them up at Barcelona airport and went on to have a fabulous holiday together. I had made good friends with an American guy called John Mason. A celebrated journalist who had flown all over the world as a reporter for The New Yorker and Newsweek. John and his partner Luis had press passes and were able to take us to places in Barcelona that were closed to the public which was a great honour.

They also arranged for a special lunch at el Quatre Gats a famous restaurant in Barcelona and told the maitre de I was the guest of honour. This meant that when the fish dish came out, a huge thing on an enormous platter I was offered the head to eat first as this was a great delicacy. All the staff lined up at the table watching while I picked around it and ate a bit, feeling very green, declared it delicious and they clapped. This amused John and Luis no end.

They were very kind to my parents and we all had a memorable trip and a good rest away from business.

We thoroughly enjoyed being free and not tied down to a business. Most jobs you can go home at 5pm or lock up and go home. You can't do that in the pub/restaurant game.

I had some lovely lunch and dinner parties on our balcony in Kemp Town looking out to sea. I adored that flat, it really made me feel I had achieved something.

However I knew if I wanted to move on I had to sell it to achieve one of my other ambitions. So 6 months after we had left the club I put the flat on the market.

Property prices had gone through the roof in the last year and seafront property in Brighton was very sort after, especially with London buyers looking for weekend places or investment opportunities. For once I knew I was going on the market at the right time.

While I was signing the forms for the estate agent, I had had the television on mute in the background. She said look at this! As I looked up I watched this plane fly into the twin towers in New York. The date I decided to sell was September 11th 2001.

Everything came to a halt after 9/11 the whole world was in shock. It affected everything and everybody. The world grew nervous especially the financial markets.

I didn't get a bite on the flat sale for 5 months. Once things calmed down a bit after 9/11 the market picked up again and prices started to soar once more.

I got two offers for the flat on the same day from two couples who just both happened to be from Primrose Hill in London. How funny was that?

Both were cash buyers and both offered the asking price.

Who do you pick in that situation? The ones who seemed the nicest is the answer. Mind you neither couple were particularly great.

I picked one.

We had decided to buy a purpose built flat in Hove.

Every flat we looked at someone beat us to it. The market was frantic and sometimes we were on our way to view flats and the agents would ring and say don't bother coming the flat has sold an hour ago. It was madness, of course the prices kept rising daily now and I thought damn it we are not going to make it.

Eventually we bought a two bedroomed flat in a purpose built block near Palmeira Square. It was central Hove where we wanted to be. Near to the shops and seafront.

It was meant to be a temporary stop gap as we were not thrilled with the block. But we were desperate so we thought we'll stay 6 months and we will move on. We stayed 15 years.

Bill and I El Portet Alicante

Brenda and Ged

Colin, John, Trevor, me, Robert and Chipmunk.

Colin and David Raven Sitges 2017

Colin and Gilly

Colin, Eileen, Freddie Forman me and Janice

Eileen White Rottingdean Club

Gary and Mike

Gary Marion Karen Merritt, Mike KEvin and Carol
Brown Gary Brown. Colins 80th prep

Gilly at Victor Spinetti's

Jeff Colin and Bill polop

Karen and Jane Prior my oldest friends.

Lesely and Peter Barrett.

Mark and neil me lolly tony fergus and jeff

Me an gilly

Me and Swales   Me and tracy at jeans

Me, Jane, Lesley and Karen Prior

Skinny with swales

Terrie Varley at Marine Parade

The Priors

Trevor Rainbow, Joanie, John Walker and
Gillian Burns

Winter palace luxor

With Eileen

With Ettie and Swales

With Gary and Marion

With jean Hirigoyen in simi Greece

With Karen and Alan Merritt

59

VIVA ESPANA

The plan had been to buy a cheaper property in Hove and use the rest to buy a Villa in Spain.

Before we had sold the seafront flat we had flown out to Alicante and fell in love with a new development that was being built in the mountains behind Benidorm on the Costa Blanca on an Urbanization called Sierra Cortina (not named after the car but translated means mountain curtain) near a traditional village/town called Finestrat.

It meant buying off plan and paying in installments. We didn't rush into it, we went and looked at lots of places, but we couldn't find anywhere to beat this place. Some of the houses were built and you could see how nice they were. Beautifully designed with staggering views down to the Mediterranean sea, with Benidorm in the distance looking like Manhattan at night, up to the Puig Campana Mountains behind us, plus lake style and size communal swimming pools and tennis courts. So we engaged a Spanish lawyer and put a deposit down and bought a holiday home in Spain.

When we got back to England we told our friends Gary and Mike (the ones I'd met in the Canaries years before) they flew over the next week and bought one too. They were going to be living the other side of the pool to us and would arrive a year after us when their house would be completed.

This was all planned on my assumption that we would sell the seafront flat quickly and for a huge profit. When I signed the forms for the villa I didn't think a bunch of mad terrorists would fly a plane into the Twin towers in New York and create havoc.

So, after we had had the offer on the seafront flat we had to fly out to Spain to sign some more legal papers. While we were there sitting on the seafront in Benidorm having a drink celebrating, the phone went and it was our English estate agent saying that the couple who were buying the seafront flat were pulling out! My stress levels went through the roof.

The guy was having some business problems and was only buying our flat for his wife to have a project and a bolt hole. So bang, all our dreams looked like sliding away plus a large chunk of money we had just put down on the Spanish house.

Within a week, a week of sleepless nights and worry, the sale was back on but only on the condition that we would move out in 6 weeks. They wanted a quick sale for cash so it meant we had 6 weeks to find somewhere else and move.

I should never have agreed to it in hindsight. A normal sale takes at least three months, but I thought oh well we are now cash buyers too it should be easy, it wasn't. It took three weeks to find somewhere and then another three weeks to complete. To do it in three weeks and move in proved very challenging. I had to pay through the nose for the solicitor to prioritise the sale. It was Bullying really they were not desperate to move in 6 weeks they had a mansion in Primrose hill for god's sake.

Still we did it. We had sold the Club, Sold the seafront flat, bought a Villa in Spain and bought a flat in Hove all within 6 months. I do not recommend it!

We now got settled into the Hove flat and started making some changes. It had been recently renovated inside so we were quite lucky but a new bathroom was needed and some cosmetic changes made but it soon became very comfortable.

We loved the central location of the flat, we didn't have a sea view unfortunately but that was the compromise to free up some cash. I loved walking our dog Bertie down to Regency Palmeira Square and through Adelaide crescent down to the beach. Plus we found another home from home, a little pub off of Western Road called the 'Bow Street Runner' owned by an old friend Robbie where we spent many happy hours over the next few years. I still held a few Sunday soirees. Terrie Varley came occasionally but I didn't entertain like I used to.

So now settled in Hove and very happy with our choice, we had lovely neighbours and the best thing about this flat was you could not hear anybody walking about above you or below it was really peaceful. It had a south facing balcony and the flat was full of light.

Now we could concentrate on Spain.

I had planned to rent the house out in Spain while we were not using it and started setting up a company I would eventually call Placido Holidays (meaning tranquil)

However, before we got to this stage we took a year to go to computer lessons. We were both computer illiterate in 2001. We had never learned at school due to our ages. Then never had the time or the inclination to use one.

Now I knew it was going to be vital. Email was the new must have communication tool.

So we went and did a proper office course. Learning about spread sheets everything and we both passed with flying colours. I could type which was a great advantage. All those years banging out the quick brown fox jumps over the lazy dog on my mother's old upright typewriter came in handy.

We also did a year's Spanish language course twice a week, as we were determined not to arrive in Spain, without being able to speak the language. We got to Intermediate stage but by then the house was built and it was ready to move over there, so the classes came to an end. Which was a shame as we both enjoyed it and were getting on very well with the difficult to learn language.

For a year we had popped over at various times to see the progress of our house being built. It was so exciting. We would sneak in on a Sunday when there were no builders about and see what was going on. I hid some pound coins for luck into the cavities before the builders plastered over.

Buying a property in Spain is a deep learning curve. Buying off plan like we did even more so. I love the Spanish but they think in a completely different way to us. They do not do Logic.

Plus because I had the cash I wanted to pay the balance of the money at the end. But no, they wanted it in installments and they wanted me to have a mortgage. I said "I don't want or need one", "Ah but you must have one to make the payments" I refused. The bank they picked actually charged you for paying money in. So imagine you are sending over 30k for an installment and then the bank you send the money to wants to charge you 10% for the privilege. They take 3 grand! So if you are spending 100k the bank wants approximately 10k just to accept the money, nobody tells you things like that. I flatly refused. Luckily my Spanish Lawyer sorted it out. We nearly lost the house over this. I was livid.

I paid a middle payment and an end one. I opened a bank account in Spain of my own choosing and let them deal with the transfers with no charges!

We had bought through an English property company that flies you out and pays for accommodation etc. We just used them for the free flights at first, but they were helpful so we let them handle our deal. It wasn't somewhere they had shown us, their properties were all down in Torrevieja further south which we didn't like at all. They open a bank account on your behalf. They don't tell you that some banks charge you for paying money in. The property companies probably get paid a commission from the banks for introducing you so you need your wits about you at all times.

Luckily we put the original deposit down in Pesetas but by the time it was ready for completion Spain had joined the Euro. To smooth the transition the rate of exchange was excellent, about 1.69 euro to the pound. So we did well out of that. Other people got really stung if their houses were completed on the next phase. The Euro had dropped so the completions often ended up costing £15+k more. What do you do if you haven't got it? A lot of people got stung.

Lots of things happen like that, things you don't think about while you are shivering on your UK couch in the winter watching "A Place in the Sun" thinking, one day!

Another is Community charges. If you buy on urbanization in Spain (a private housing estate) the "community" runs the estate. The builders will tell you that they estimate the community charges will be 600 Euros a year. Whatever they tell you double or treble it. Plus Rates (SUMA) and local taxes.

The day came when we were due to move over. This was in February 2002. We piled the car up and the dog Bertie and drove down to Spain.

We drove across the Massif Central in France in a blizzard with no snow tyres; it took us 3 days and were using maps. Sat Nav didn't exist then.

Hair raising at times it was an adventure. The French Roads are marvelous once you get out of the cities. Driving from the French border on the A7 through Spain the countryside is quite flat and feature less. However as soon as you get near Valencia it changes. The Costa Blanca is a beautiful region and as soon as we saw the orange groves and the almond blossom we knew we were nearly "home" Dramatic mountainous landscapes surrounded by fruit trees and blossom. The Costa Blanca is the garden of Spain like Kent is to England.

Tired but excited and pumped full of adrenalin we went to the office of Murcia Puchades to collect the key. They don't give you long to make a snag list. You have to try and find out any faults on your property very quickly. We had quite a few issues but nothing like some of my neighbours eventually had.

However they were pretty good and sorted most things out eventually. We were only the second couple to move in onto the new part of the development and we were next to the show house, so it was in their interest to make it look good.

The pool wasn't finished and was full of rubbish but we were told that it would be finished soon.

However the first night was freezing cold. There was snow on the mountains behind our house. We had done a deal with the English property company that instead of one of their naf furniture packages they would give us a voucher to pick out what we wanted from a designated shop.

We had used this to buy decent beds which had been delivered. However with no heating it was too cold to get into bed. So we spent the first night in the kitchen sleeping on two sun loungers fully clothed with duvets over us, wooly hats and gloves on and the oven turned up high. Luckily we had asked them to arrange to connect the electric and gas otherwise we would have had nothing!

The next day we went straight out and bought electric fan heaters.

Furniture shops were very few and far between then in our area and we had to drive over to Albir and Altea for furniture shops. Luckily we found a nice one with stylish furniture, it was not Spanish. Spanish furniture is awful.

This was probably Norwegian. Anyway, we bought a king size good quality sofa bed and two arm chairs in a blue and white stripped fabric and these were delivered the next day.

This is one of the great things in Spain. Service, you don't have to wait months for delivery of goods like we do in the UK. If you buy a fridge freezer it will arrive the same or next day and the men will put it where you want and plug it in ready to go. No extra charge.

So within no time we were furnished. Our neighbour's Malcolm and Phyllis who had moved in just before us told us where to go to get a great bargain TV. I had dozens of video tapes I had brought over to watch, so we were soon feeling at home.

The house soon looked lovely; we had a big garden that looked straight down to the sea. I could lie in bed in the mornings and look at the Mediterranean and the usually clear blue sky. We had a roof top terrace to sunbathe on. Eventually the pool was finished and the grounds tidied up enough to look welcoming.

I was determined to be positive and get involved in Spanish life.

We had to go to the first community meeting to discuss finance budgets. I went with my lawyer and my new bank manager Archie who had become a great friend. (I don't know what I would have done without him in those early days). Not knowing the format I put on a black Armani suit and a black tee shirt. When we arrived we sat in the front row. Being a bit deaf I have to sit near the front to hear anything. It was all in rapid Spanish so it didn't really matter although they did have an English translator there who didn't say much. Luckily Archie and my lawyer were able to keep me up to speed.

It was a long meeting with lots of questions and complaints and some angry yelling from disgruntled home buyers. This is normal.

Afterwards I was told we had put the building company on their toes as they thought we were all lawyers (Abogados in Spanish) sitting in the front in our suits. And it made them very careful how they responded. Two of my new neighbour's who were to become lifelong friends Gary and Marion Evans thought we were the mafia. We all had a good laugh about it later on.

I eventually sat on this residents committee for 5 years. You give up in the end as it's a thankless task. Nothing ever gets done without a big fight.

My advice to anyone thinking of doing it. Rent! or buy somewhere that is not part of a community or on an urbanization, like in a village. Even a flat works on the same community run principle. Some people never pay their community fees and it's really hard to get them to pay up.

I could fill another book about the dos and don'ts of buying in Spain but others have already done it. Just do your homework. I thought I had but there is loads you do not expect.

I also was introduced to the local Mayor and became friendly. He was very keen to get the (Estrangers) British, Dutch, and Belgian etc neighbour's views on how to develop Finestrat. In 2000 it was still an undeveloped little village quite poor in funds. Now it's in a much better situation regarding sanitation and infrastructure then it was then. This is due to the amount of building in the area. Not everyone approves, but without it these people would not have had a decent sewage system or safe electricity and good schools and doctors.

I was able to be involved long enough to get a roundabout placed at the entrance to our urbanization which was a "thrill" every time you pulled out of it praying nothing was coming at you at 90 miles an hour from both directions, and a new bus stop but that was about it. We were never able to increase the amount of buses that stayed at about 4 a day, if they turned up at all. We could never get one to come into the urbanization either. The council figured if you could afford a house in Sierra Cortina you could afford a car! The environment was not a big factor in Spanish minds then.

We attended some great "Do's" at Finestrat town hall. Nobody knows how to party like the Spanish. After that our friendly Mayor got knocked out in the local elections and the new one who got elected in on a manifesto to supply all men over 50 (I kid you not) with free Viagra. Large billboards all over Finestrat were erected forgive the pun, advertising his generous offer.

That was the extent of his generosity; he turned out to be a bit of a big prick funnily enough and lost out next time due to corruption charges, also common in Spain.

So I did my bit for our community. Largely people don't want to get involved and are happy to leave it to others to do all the work, but they are the first to complain when things go wrong. In the end and on our third lot of managing agents I left the committee. Finding a managing estate agent in Spain who is not on the fiddle is challenging.

60

PLACIDO HOLIDAYS

I had my First guest booked for May. We had decided to live in Spain from December 27th until the end of March. Get away from English winters. I never regretted it a bit, the rest of the time it was available to rent for holidays.

I did well with holiday lettings over the years. I had a very reliable team in place in Spain that stayed with me for 15 years. Without reliable back up in place it's impossible. Don't even think about it unless you have. Also you need to speak a bit of Spanish.

There's a lot of work goes into running a holiday lettings business especially one that's overseas. Lots of hours dealing with enquires that don't go anywhere, lots of time wasters etc, on the plus side I could run this from home sitting down at a desk. Over the years 90 %of our guests were delightful. I never met them. Julie my rep in Spain took over when they arrived.

You'll never make a lot of money out of it either, You have lots of expenses, main ones being cleaners and reps (meeters and greeters) Then there is maintenance, laundry costs and replacement, advertising and taxes, plus electricity, gas, water, community fees, rates and local taxes etc.

We made enough to cover the bills, pay me a small wage and pay for our winters out there. We were lucky; you have to pick the right property and location if you want to do that. Even we were a bit out of the way for some, you needed a car, but it suited families which was my target market. I never let to groups of all same sex groups or youngsters.

Colin did all the maintenance jobs. Each year there was work to do when we got back. Touching up paintwork, repairing broken items replacing bedding and towels. Once we had done that then we could relax and enjoy it, and we did a lot.

Our Spanish had been helpful but not as much as I had hoped. Once you start dealing with local builders, electricians and plumbers you realise none of them speak Castilian which is what you learn in Britain and in our case they spoke Valenciano. What with that and most Spanish people willing to practice their English to speak to you, it's easy to get lazy about it. It is a difficult language to learn, I'm ok in a bar or restaurant or for asking directions but that's about it, now I've forgotten so much. However, you need it to really integrate.

I made quite a few Spanish friends over the years. You often hear some British people quite snootily say, "Oh the British never bother to speak the local language. They never want to eat foreign food, all they want is English Breakfasts and chips with everything". While there is a small element like that I find it to be untrue in the main.

These people do not consider that maybe the Spanish do not want to integrate with lots of foreigners moving into their villages and towns either. They are no different to us in that respect, they like their own tribes and culture just as much as the rest of us. Generally though if you make an effort, they are a very friendly, generous and welcoming race of people.

Spanish friends in the hotel industry there tell me that the British are the best at "trying" whether it's just Buenos Dias or Hola or por favor and gracias, they try. The worst apparently are the French. Apparently they make no effort to converse at all.

We are also the best at trying foreign cuisines. The diverse choice of restaurants in England proves that. On the contrary you rarely see a Spanish, French or Italian person sampling foreign food. They stick to what they like and drink their own wine to. You very rarely see imported wines and food items in Spanish shops and never on menus. So perhaps we should be kinder to ourselves. I can say first hand you do miss English bacon and teabags and marmite and all those things. Luckily in places like the Costa's you can buy your home comforts easily now. It's the Spanish that seem to like chips with everything anyway.

We had decided on the Costa Blanca after a holiday to Benidorm, several years earlier. I had never considered Benidorm as somewhere to have a holiday I didn't think it was my type of place.

Terrie Varley swore by it and went twice a year there with her "Varley tours" groups of friends from Brighton. They all loved it. I never fancied it. I'd spent many enjoyable holidays in Torremolinos and Marbella on the Costa del Sol as Colin's Brother Bill used to live in Torre.

Sitges was my place, once I went there I never wanted to go anywhere else. It was and is an up market area. Known as the St Tropez of Spain, after everyone kept telling me how great Benidorm was I decided to go.

Swales and I went for our winter break there after New Year, instead of the Canaries. Well that was the start of a long love affair.

We had such a good time and we never stopped laughing.

The beaches were beautiful. We stayed in the old town where there was a lively gay scene. The streets were lined with fantastic tapas bars and great shops, what's not to like? One night we did venture down into the new town. Now we could see where all the negativity came from regarding Benidorm.

The Square known as little England is really little Britain. Lots of British, Irish, Scottish and Welsh bars. They are there to capture the Brits and Irish who like a pint of vodka and red bull for breakfast for 2 Euros. Now days its Hen party central and best avoided.

There are some excellent clubs down there though. One we liked back then was The Town. They used to book top acts and it was a really good night out. But it has a completely different atmosphere to the old town.

Benidorm is a massive place however made up of different districts. The Square as it is known is one tiny little bit of it. The rest of it is great.

The high rises put some people off, but when Benidorm was invented as a holiday resort and to provide much needed employment by the mayor Pedro Zargozo Orts. The high rise blocks of flats were built to house the work force for the hundreds of hotels. It is still Spain's busiest most popular resort, with the Spanish. It is busy all year around because of its fantastic micro climate.

Colin went out there with Swales and he also loved it. So when we retired after we had our month in Sitges we flew out to Benidorm and stayed with Phillip (The Duchess of Benidorm) in his brand new boutique style bnb called Casa Don Juan, right in the heart of the old town while we were house hunting. He made us so welcome and remains a friend nearly 20 years later.

The fabulous winter weather and the all year round buzz made up our mind to settle near Benidorm and that's how we ended up in Finestrat about three miles outside. I didn't want to buy in Benidorm itself as its too noisy. Fine for a holiday but not for a home, for us anyway.

I really wanted Sitges too, but Sitges is the most expensive area of Spain. Plus it only has a short season and is very cold in the winter. At lot colder than Benidorm.

So we started our other life in Spain. We loved it. La Cala Finestrat is the bay. Finestrat village is a couple of miles north and we were situated in the middle.

La Cala had an old fashioned uncomercialised feel to it then and we loved it. There was a small pretty bay with a few bars restaurants and shops. Looking inland there was a car park and fields. You wouldn't recognise it now; The whole area was built on as blocks of flats shot up in the boom years. However it has been done nicely with wide avenues and nice bars and restaurants. That land was owned by neighbouring town La vila Joyosa which was also terribly poor and in need of funds. The building of these flats meant that La vila could be transformed and indeed it was, they even have a theatre and Opera house now. It's a beautiful resort.

It was my parents golden wedding anniversary and we persuaded them to celebrate it in La Cala with us. They wanted the family there so I found them a lovely three bedroom apartment in the bay with sea views. Deborah Brian and the kids all flew over and moved in with mum and dad. My parents also loved La Cala and Benidorm my father would have stayed forever I think.

For their big night I booked a table for 8 at the Benidorm Palace. A huge venue on the outskirts of Benidorm. The shows are legendary with bare breasted Las Vegas style girls with masses of Ostrich feathers. The ticket price included Dinner and Wine (lots of it then) It was a Good 4 course meal that included smoked salmon king prawns and fillet steak. It is a wonderful night out with lots of international variety acts. The costumes and choreography are second to none.

We were all really looking forward to it. I'd taken mum and dad up there to pick a table and pay the deposit. The morning of their anniversary I got a phone call from the box office to say they were cancelling the show that night and we could either have a refund or pick another night.

I was livid. I said my parents have flown my whole family out here, paid for flights accommodation especially for their golden wedding what do you mean your cancelling why?

It turned out the local Mayor was being given some award from the tourist board and wanted it presented it to him in a large enough venue to match his ego.

So he commandeered the whole of the Benidorm Palace which seats 1'660 people on a whim for his presentation. He gave them no notice and they had to give into him. Mayors are all powerful there, that's why I don't agree with them here.

There was nothing I could do. When I told my mother she was in tears. So disappointed, as was my father. Her tears soon turned to rage and she made us take her over there.

We got hold of the owner a Spaniard who has a British wife. A nice couple to be fair, they offered another night and complimentary flowers for the table. My Mother told them what she thought of that! We ended up with a complimentary table the next night with extra champagne all on the house. My parents could not get over how a mayor could do that.

So to salvage the actual anniversary I booked a table for dinner down in the bay. After our meal we strolled past a very busy bar we hadn't tried yet. It looked the liveliest so we went inside, outside being full. The Waiters were great, we were made so welcome. When we left many hours later, they brought us all a drink on the house and Deborah and Brian got a bottle of Cava to take home. I was so impressed with the service here; it became our "local" We drank there for the next fifteen years. The Marina bar was now headquarters, we all used to meet up there for hours of fun.

The next day we went off to the Benidorm Palace and we did have the most fantastic night. My nephew Jonathan's eyes were out on stalks at all the bare breasts on show (Ala Follies Bergere)

61

ONE FOR THE ROAD

The Marina bar is owned by two brothers Pepe and Antonio. The service is second to none. They employ properly trained Spanish waiters. In Spain you have to go to training school to get a bar/ waiting diploma, you can't just walk in off the street and get a bar job. So we got very spoiled when we were wintering in La Cala.

Over the years many friendships were formed, mainly with other British ex pats but also with a lot of Dutch and Belgian people.

There was quite a large gay community based in La Cala. People like us who liked Benidorm for a night out but didn't want to live in it. There were those who lived there all year round and worked, and others who were retired or just spent the winter there like us. Sunday lunchtime /afternoon about 3pm about 30 of us used to congregate there. All ages and sexes. We had a ball and often wouldn't stagger home until 9 or 10 o'clock! 7 hour sessions. Most of us went into Benidorm on Saturday nights and didn't get home until 3 or 4 am so they were quite boozy weekends.

There is a large terrace outside the bar where we would sit and gossip and laugh, sip our beers or vodka and tonics and put the world to rights while gazing out onto the sandy beach and the seashore. Usually sunny in the winter in the day time we would peel of layers and bask in the sun. As the sun started to go down we would witness some of the most beautiful sunsets you could wish to see. Then the coats would go back on and one of the guys would wheel out the patio heaters. It gets chilly at night in Spain between November and April.

It never mattered in the Marina bar if you had 2 drinks or 10 as soon as you paid your bill they would bring you one for the road. (On the house) This could be fatal if you were trying to be good. Inevitably some friends would arrive and join you and you'd end up having a couple more and then another bill and another "one for the road" Antonio and Pepe were not stupid. However, it was a lovely gesture and one that has made sure that they are always busy.

However it wasn't all sitting in the sun boozing. We got into the lifestyle and lived there as we would at home just in the sun (mostly) Colin was taken seriously ill once or twice and was hospitalised. I got attacked by a Rottweiler dog when I was out walking Bertie and he broke my arm. The care and attention we received was second to none. The Spanish healthcare system can on some levels put ours to shame. However with my broken arm they tried to charge me, even though I had my European E111 card. The administration at the hospital did not like it one bit that they had to claim the money back from the UK.

However on the whole like with Colin they were marvelous and the healthcare was free. We always took out 90 day health insurance as well just in case.

Everything in Spain involves reams of paperwork and the manana saying is true. Even just to pay your rates (The Suma) or get the car MOT'd could take the best part of a day. When shopping if you haven't got everything you want or paid your bills or been to the bank by 2pm you've had it until 5pm when everything reopens until 9pm (except the banks) Things are easier now with direct debits etc but then it was something you had to get used to. A lot of places stick to the old rules today. Lunch in Spain is at 2 o'clock.

We used to go to a local restaurant for lunch, a huge place that could sit 300 people. At 2pm all the Spanish come through the door, lots of workman, business men, and families. They would and us have a 3 course meal including wine for 9 Euros. About £7.50. Then go somewhere for a siesta then back to work at 5pm or 6pm.

The Spanish are a hard working race and would work up until 9pm or 10pm at night.

We used to drive all over the coast and the country side looking for new places to eat. There are some really gastronomic finds in the area.

Paella comes from Valencia so we were in the region for that but also the most delicious shoulders of lamb roasted slowly in garlic and rosemary. If you like oranges you can buy a big bag of them, 5 kilos for 3 Euros about £2.00

The seafood is spectacular and we developed a real liking for Octopus and Squid. Most 'menu Del Dias' (menu of the day) serves grilled sole on the bone as an option too.

All restaurants in Spain have to offer a 'menu del dia 'by law. A fixed price 3 course meal usually with wine or beer. This is usually offered at lunchtime, which is when the Spanish tend to have their main meal of the day.

So for three months every year we would go out at least twice a week sometimes three for lunch. We would seek out places in Alicante province where some of Spain's finest restaurants reside or drive up into the mountains and go to country restaurants with log lit fireplaces. If it was very warm we would sit by the sea in Altea or Moraira and spend two hours over lunch.

On the way back sometimes we stopped at the Marina bar for sundowners before we went home to watch TV or sleep.

For the first few years I went back into my old habit of entertaining and doing the Sunday soirees. We might meet some friends at the marina bar then I'd bring them all back for Sunday lunch/dinner and the records would go on after the meal and a party. Sometimes if it was warm enough I'd have people for the day and do lunch for 16 in the garden it was fun.

Colin had bumped into one of his old navy chums Graham who became part of the crowd. He moved out to Benidorm from Southampton looking for a better life in the sun. Graham had a very droll sense of humour, he could either be a pain in the arse or very funny.

Sadly after a few years he developed a brain tumour and died. Lots of us from Spain attended his funeral in Southampton. Apparently there had been a right old hoo ha because his last wish was to have a very well endowed male stripper perform in the chapel of rest instead of Hymns.

Anyway the Chapel of rest wouldn't give in so they had to make do with some nice songs and a few jokes.

After at the wake the stripper had been booked and after we all got settled he started his act. I must say his member was huge. Graham would have loved it. Guess who he came up to first to feel it! He tried to drag me up onstage but my back was playing up so I sent my mate Gary up to do the honour's instead. It was one of the best funerals I've been to it was such a laugh. Which of course is what Graham intended.

One of my favourite villages in the mountains was a place with the unfortunate name of Polop. We got to know Polop through bumping in to an old friend of ours from Brighton, Mark Allen Foord and his partner Neil Spencer in Benidorm. They told us they had bought a bar in a mountain village about 30 minutes from Benidorm in a place called Polop we laughed at the name.

We went up to see them once they had settled in. It was a lovely bar, an old inn called La Font. A traditional village bar that served Tapas, a large room with a big log fire.

We thought they were mad, but Mark spoke a bit of Spanish and had lived in Spain before. His mother and late father had a small holding in the Jalon valley close by.

They did very well for a few years. It soon became a regular haunt for us. If the weather was cold or a bit bleak we would head up to Polop on Sunday lunchtime and huddle around the log fire. Long lunches that were great fun. They soon attracted a British following including again quite a few gay couples that lived in or near the village.

We made several very good friends up there. It is a very pretty village with great character and beautiful views.

It is one of the success stories of integration. The Brits I knew here mixed with the Spanish and got involved in the local Fiestas and every year we went to the street Paella cooking competition. Where family's cook on open fires placed around the edges of the village square. In the centre are long trestle tables under canopies for everyone to sit and eat.

The beer is free provided by the local council! After the competition is judged, everyone sits down to eat the paellas. Music strikes up and the party starts. Children take it in turns to dare each other to jump over the dying flames of the fires. (EU rules regarding health and safety don't mean a thing in rural Spain)

These fiestas can last a week. They always involve lots of processions, music, brass bands, plenty of alcohol, lots of foods and masses of fireworks. The Spanish love fireworks. It's not so much the spectacle as the noise, the louder the bang the better.

There are 366 fiestas a year in Benidorm alone. Some very small but some like the Moors and Christians or the Three Kings parades at Christmas are huge and spectacular. One of my favourites is the burying of the sardine on the beach! It symbolises the burying of the past and allows everyone to have a fresh start, this takes place on Ash Wednesday.

My British/Scottish friends Bill and Pete and others introduced a charity bed race. They were trying to take over an old school building and do it up to provide a place for children with learning difficulties. In Spain unfortunately children born who are not "normal" are still something that seems to cause shame within families. They protect and look after them but they are not "put on show" as such.

So, to raise money for the school the Brits started the bed race charging around the village in old beds on wheels. The Spanish thought this was hilarious and really appealed to their sense of fun and they joined in. I'm pleased to say this continues every year and the Brits and others in Polop were able to re open this old school for disabled and disadvantaged children.

Charity shops and fundraising events are few and far between in Spain, which I always found odd for such a Catholic country, any you do come across are inevitably run or organised by ex pat Brits.

In egypt group

John B John Mason, me Luis sitges

Legs up poniente

Lunch garden spain

Marina bar group

Marina bar One for the road.

Mum dad and me albir

My view from bed in spain   Our house in spain

Our house in the corner spain

Our local beach in Spain La cala finestrat

View of benidorm from our sitting room

62

Psychic Healing

I can't remember how it came about but I started doing my old party piece of dukering or palm reading up in Polop. For some time I'd also developed a skill for healing. I've always been a bit psychic and interested in Spiritualism. I am what they call clairaudient. Where you can tune into voices and atmosphere but can't visualise like a clairvoyant does. Although I had seen that ghost of a man in The Rottingdean club years before.

I had been doing quite a bit of healing with hands for the past few years and had had some good success with it. A lady in Polop always tells me I cured her very painful sciatica from her shoulder.

The problem with healing is you need to know how to get rid of the pain. I'm not sure I did and took some of other people's pain on board. I no longer do this.

One Sunday afternoon I was doing a bit of after lunch palm reading, these were more than fortune tellings. I used to really tune into the person and they turned into counseling sessions and I could talk about health matters and love affairs all sorts. Once people realised I knew what I was doing they opened up to me and I hope I was able to offer comfort. I never charged or asked for anything in return.

Two men walked over to me and they said would you mind doing ours? Afterwards they introduced themselves to me (I never ask names or questions before a reading) as Lawrence (lolly) and

Tony. I said I've heard of you! Are you friends with Gary and Mike? "Yes we met them on a cruise a few months ago" so small world. Anyway, after I had given them both a reading they told me that they owned a psychic help line. Lolly had also worked as a clairvoyant and had so impressed one of his clients he had set him up in business with a psychic phone line service and it had been a tremendous success. Lolly and Tony were impressed with my reading and offered me a job on the spot. I declined I wasn't interested in doing it professionally.

We became good friends. Lolly had been a Missionary when he left Oxford with a degree in theology. He has a strong Christian ethic. He has plowed back profits from his psychic service into poor countries like India and has created and maintained a village there.

They have a large villa near Polop and we went to lots of pool parties there over the next few years. We became close friends. They were always on at me to work for them from home doing readings over the phone.

Eventually I agreed to do it for 6 months. For so many hours in the evening I would be available to give readings. I got paid for this. Lots of people criticise these phone lines but in my short experience I realised they actually give people a lot of comfort and hope.

You obviously can't see the client and it takes a while to build up the ability to be able to offer readings in this way. I took to it quite easily. The clients varied enormously from people suffering bereavement to barristers asking for advice regarding case work. I'm not going to disclose anymore except to say I'm glad to have helped lots of people in distress. I was able to provide an address regarding a murder enquiry that proved accurate and I was able to comfort people dealing with grief. I had a lot of regular callers as well as some nutcase's as well.

One very funny one was from a woman in Dorset who rang me three times in one week. She had a strong Dorset burr. Apparently her husband was always pestering her for sex. (Nothing to do with psychic reading, she just wanted a chat) "he's always rubbing himself up against me dear, doesn't matter if I'm washing up or feeding the chickens, up he comes rubbing his todger against my back, I'm right fed up with it I really am" Oh dear I said trying not to burst out laughing, where is he now. "In church dear....pause, he's the Vicar! True story.

I gave it up after 6 months as I felt it was too demanding. It can be quite depressing as well as uplifting but 6 months was enough for me.

However this didn't affect our friendship. Lolly and Tony can be very generous and invited 16 of us on to a cruise around the Caribbean and we often went sailing on their yacht. We had a marvelous time in the Caribbean. My first cruise and it definitely gave me the bug to do more, and we have.

So through a chance meeting in a street in Benidorm we made many friends in this mountain village called Polop. Some good friendships that last to this day.

Unfortunately Mark and Neil sold the bar after about 5 years and went back to the UK. Mark sadly died very young aged 42 through alcohol related problems. It was very sad as he had not touched a drop for over a year and was working as a councillor to others with addiction problems, but the damage had been done.

We attended his funeral in Manchester and then a few months' later lots of us flew out to Spain and Neil scattered his ashes from the top of the village of Polop overlooking the Jalon valley. It was a beautiful day and we returned him to the place he always regarded as home and where he was his happiest.

63

WOULD YOU LIKE TO TASTE THIS?

After I had got Placido holidays set up and we were settled back in Hove. I got bored after a few years of retirement I was now 45. So I got myself a part time job as a food and wine demonstrator for a company called REL and they had a contract with Waitrose to supply demonstrators like me to promote their offers in-store.

I really enjoyed this job. I was basically back behind a bar dealing with the public serving food and drinks like I always had done and showing off. I finally settled in their Worthing store and I stayed for 5 years.

I built up a good rapport with the staff or partners as John Lewis and Waitrose workers are called and the customers. I had lots of regulars, many were elderly people that used to come in just for a chat, this was sad but I always had time for them and give them extra big measures to taste. If I liked people I would often give them several "tastes" and Saturday afternoons turned into a mini club in the shop and often customers would get to the check out quite pissed! But laden with wine bottles in their trolley.

I enjoyed this because basically I was my own boss. I turned these demonstration tables into elaborate affairs with fresh flower displays and handed out snacks to draw people to the table. After a couple of years I just concentrated on the wine tables and promoted wines and spirits from all the different countries and regions. I'm pleased to say that I had the best sales record for anyone at REL for wine sales.

I often had loads left over so I used to take it home and give Colin a wine tasting indoors. (I was supposed to tip it down the sink, disgraceful waste!) We never wanted for any booze for a few years.

The other upside of this job was that I was on a zero hours contract, which meant I was self employed, no sick pay or holiday pay but it meant I could say every year I can only work until Christmas, I'm going to Spain and I'll come back in the spring.

The downside to this job was one, the phone in and paper work after you got off of the shop floor. It became more and more complicated and detailed each year and was a pain in the butt. The other was the standing. You stand in more or less the same spot for 7-8 hours a day/ I was doing 4-5 days a week. At some stage, this little part time job was turning into a full time one. My right ankle used to be so swollen when I got home that I would have to keep it raised with a bag of frozen peas on it to reduce the swelling.

My back problem had returned and was giving me pain on and off as well. I eventually went to the hospital where I was given physiotherapy for two years. Useless! I kept asking for an MRI scan, but was told it's too expensive. When I did eventually get one it turned out I had no ligament in my right ankle at all. The doctors were amazed I had been able to walk or stand for hours at all.

I had the sort of injury usually associated with a professional sportsman, which gave my friends and family a good laugh. When I told them what I had done and was doing for a living they said Ah that explains it. Too many hours standing on hard floors (all those meals, weddings and buffets years ago)

Anyway, I had to undergo two operations for this, the first one didn't work. It was very unpleasant and I had to be in a moon boot for several months both times.

It was painful and difficult to wash etc. Colin had to help me strip wash on a bar stool (appropriately) at the sink.

With my back they found out I have a condition known as facet joint syndrome and I had 32+ injections in my spine and special shoe lifts and a corset made for me.

Obviously I couldn't work anymore. REL's contract was coming to an end with Waitrose anyway.

For the next two years I had to walk with a stick or crutches. I was in agony a lot. No pain killers worked even tramadol (morphine) the only thing that did help was Vodka. Shame you have to go through the hangovers and other side effects that go with it!

My back problem had obviously become worse because of my ankle condition. I still spent a fortune on chiropractors and osteopaths there was only so much the NHS could do and they don't offer treatments that really work anyway. I tried them all. In Spain I found a doctor who would give me epidural injections in the spine that they use for child birth which helped a bit.

Eventually after several years and lots of money spent, I found a clinic in Benidorm that offered manipulation, massage and electronic acupuncture. In Spain it's great that you can go to a clinic and get combination therapy from the same person. It's not just one thing or the other as it is in the UK.

This Clinic was not very expensive 30 euros for an hour's therapy. After a few sessions I was able to get off the table and walk out of there, and throw away the walking stick! I believe the combination therapy worked but especially the electronic acupuncture.

The relief was immense. I went back every year for "maintenance" Once you've got a bad back you have it for life, plus there is no cure for facet joint syndrome, you have to live with it, but since then I've only had to use a stick once or twice.

While I was more or less house bound for months and over the next two years I decided to take an online journalism course. I've always been interested in writing. It was hard slog but eventually I got through the course and obtained a diploma in journalism. I never really intended to do much with it. It was just a hobby. With the internet turning everyone into a blogger it's a hard career to crack.

One thing I did do for a while was write up the theatre reviews for the New Venture Theatre in Brighton. A prestigious amateur dramatic theatre set up by Laurence Olivier and Vivien Leigh. It showcases new works by new authors. I enjoyed this and did it until I moved out of the area.

64

TRAVELING

As well as the Caribbean cruise with the gang where we went to many destinations in the Windward and Leeward Islands, (the Beaches in Barbados are breathtaking) I've travelled extensively.

Another trip 16 of us from La Cala Finestrat took off for Egypt. This was an incredible experience. One week on a Nile cruise which was quite surreal. Laying on your bed watching the world go by as you sail down the river. Camels, people, clothes washing, cooking, just living. It was like a moving biblical picture. The treasures of Luxor just staggering. Like most places much better to experience in real life. The second week was spent in a purpose built luxury resort in El Gouna. Great place but everywhere we were surrounded by armed guards. This was just before the 'Arab spring' and you could definitely sense a tension in the air.

On the way back the ship stopped in Venezuela were we had a bbq lunch on one of the best beaches I've ever seen.

Colin and I have travelled all over the place and I won't bore you with a full list. From Puerto Rico to the Isle of white. My favourite places are Venice, (just beautiful) Spain... all of it, France, Egypt, and the Greek Islands especially Mykonos.

While we were in Spain we drove all over it and it never ceases to surprise. Granada is a fabulous place, so friendly and the Alhambra Palace another wonder of the world.

I went back to New York Recently and the Caribbean on a cruise for New Year with a big Gang. New York has changed since I first went. I preferred Manhattan 30 years ago. Now it's like a very, very expensive theme park, shame.

I'm happy now to potter around Europe.

65

TURNING ANOTHER PAGE

In 2016 we sold the house in Spain. We had lived there every winter for 15 years and it was time for a change. Selling like buying is an education in Spain. Luckily we made a small profit. The property boom has been over in Spain since 2012 when the Euro crashed. This period was a sad one for Spain. Since joining the Euro they had seen such gains and prosperity. The building boom had created many millionaires. Then over night bang! All gone. Youth unemployment soared and remains at 50+%. For the first time I witnessed poverty on the Costas. A soup kitchen was set up in la cala with a drop in centre to leave or buy clothes. I saw people going through the communal waste bins looking for food.

Lots of property was repossessed and sold off by the banks. Things have recovered a lot now, but I spoke to many Spanish acquaintances who wished they had never joined the Euro.

66

Bye Bye Brighton

We also put our flat in Hove on the market. After 30 years living in Brighton and Hove we no longer enjoyed it. The atmosphere has changed a lot. The Green party and the loony left, have ruined lots of it with their daft policies and political correctness.

It is now known as "Islington on sea" The property prices rocketed on the back of the London housing boom. Hipsters and left wing media types, champagne socialists bought up lots of the nicer Hove properties, after flogging their Islington houses for millions and moved to the seaside.

The shops that sell "things" slowly disappeared and dozens of organic free trade coffee shops sprang up, where the metropolitan elite and the new age house husbands gather to devour their Guardian newspapers with religious fervour, while sipping a vegan latte, and unwashed and hung-over students stare vacantly into their laptops.

Hated cars have had to make way for endless bus lanes leading to nowhere, while old 'up cycled' bikes with dangerous baby carriages on the back sway in the breeze from the seafront, transporting the gender fluid passengers to their next mindfulness and wellbeing classes.

The graffiti vandals known as "street artists" by the diversity tsars have covered every available surface with some kind of depressing illiterate scrawl. Homeless people sleep in the doorways of the declining shops and the drug problem is one of the worst in Britain.

The once vibrant gay scene has got a bit hidden beneath the hen night parties that fill some of the gay bars for tacky pre nuptial celebrations. Gay men and women stand back watching it all disappear in the name of equality and diversity.

It is still considered hip and trendy. It always was. It is still great for a day out. The seafront is now much better than it was years ago, much more fun and packed on sunny weekends. So it is not all bad certainly.

I've got to say I preferred Brighton when it was a lot less populated, when it had good shops, gangsters, actors, camp queens, dodgy antique dealers, dirty weekenders and barrow boys. When English was still the main spoken language and a child wearing a burkha was an unknown entity.

The sleazy afternoon drinking clubs were much more fun than sitting in an all day open converted boozer, sipping a kombucha tea for a tenner, and discussing climate change.

The younger generation do take themselves much more seriously than we ever did.

Being a transient city people come and go. For me the people I had loved had mainly left. Not on the back of a dodgy bike but on an express train to heaven.

I lost two of my best friends Tracy Davenport and Terrie Varley. Tracy we lost to Emphysema (caused through smoking) at the young age of 63 and Terrie due to age related dementia at 81.

These two big characters left a big hole in my life and I miss them very much. Their funerals were "events" in Brighton. Tracey was referred to in the press as "The Godmother of gay Brighton" and Terrie "the Grandmother" Hundreds gathered to pay their respects to these wonderful women.

All the others I have mentioned earlier in the book have either carried their large gin and tonics onto a cloud somewhere above the palace pier or moved along to Eastbourne.

67

WESTWARD BOUND

Colin and I had been looking for some time at properties in West Sussex about 10-15 miles further along the coast.

The idea was to get my parents a bungalow or a nice apartment in Worthing. I was happy to go as well, as I had got to know Worthing quite well during my Waitrose days and liked it.

However it never happened for them, as dad got ill and my mother got ill and her memory started to deteriorate.

We moved to Rustington by chance in December 2016 a house we were after in Worthing fell through and we looked further afield. I'm so glad we did. Rustington Littlehampton is a lovely place with a quiet beach with multi coloured beach huts, nice shops and people say good morning to each other.

For the price of our Hove flat we were able to buy a four bedroom house plus change, with a small garden so we could get another dog. Bertie had died in Spain several years before and we missed having a dog.

So we sold and moved from Spain in October and sold and moved from Hove in December, Once again we were attempting a multi move. It wasn't planned like that, events and fate took over.

Then in January I flew to New York with the gang to celebrate New Year and go on a caribbean cruise. I was exhausted; I had also had a bout of a rotten flu virus that was reoccurring. It was a nasty one and it came back on the cruise. In hindsight I should never have gone I was exhausted and weak from the flu and the stress of moving twice! And looking after and worried about my mum and dad. However, it had been booked and paid for months in advance so......

Everything went wrong from the 6 hour delay we had at the airport to me packing my passport in my suitcase and nearly not making the ship. Roaming around hell's kitchen in New York looking for accommodation on a bank holiday in the freezing cold and rain totally alone. It and I was a nightmare. One best forgotten.

68

LUCCA

I got my wish to have another dog. I typed in Shih Tzu cross puppies into Google and immediately this dear little face appeared. He was nearly 12 weeks old and ready to go. He was born in Brighton and was a 3/4 Shih Tzu and 1/4 King Charles Cavalier spaniel. I went to view him and his two sisters. He bounded over to me full of life. The other two sat at my feet, cute but quiet. The boy was full of life and I chose him and I named him Lucca because I loved the Italian name. I took him straight to the vets to check him over and he said you've got yourself a lovely little puppy there.

Lucca has brought so much joy into both of our lives. He makes us laugh. He's incredibly affectionate too. He's full of energy and is good for me as he makes me walk. We love the beach and he runs and chases the ball for hours on Rustington or West Beach in Littlehampton.

Chipmunk says to me witheringly. He's a dog not a surrogate child. But he's one of the family and we spoil him rotten. One of the best decisions I made was to get him. His besotted Godmother Gilly, leaves her St John's Wood apartment to move in and baby sit him while we are on holiday. Eileen would love to but is now also getting old. These days she is happy to stay at home in the west end of London after a life of flying around the world to glamorous destinations like Patrick Denis's character Auntie Mame.

Beautiful Bertie

lucca being bad

Lucca

lucca first haircut

Sam

69

REACHING MATURITY

I had been looking after my mum and dad a lot. First mum got very ill but then made a remarkable recovery, then dad started losing weight over a period of 3 years and despite many tests, the doctors couldn't find anything wrong with him.

When we decided to sell up in Spain, in the back of my mind I knew that I was going to be needed more at home.

Dad did improve for a while, but his once healthy appetite never really returned. He kept up his good spirits though and spent hours pottering in his garden which he loved.

We celebrated his 90th birthday on October 31st with a small champagne tea with the family at our house but he didn't look very well. A couple of days later he died.

My dear gentle, stubborn father who had hardly ever been ill in his life, never even took aspirin had just died of old age. Even though you are half expecting it, it still comes as a terrible shock.

I had a very good relationship with my father. We worked together for years in the pub and the club and never had a row. He was a good man and I loved him, I know that he loved me and he adored my mother and my sister.

Christmas that year wasn't easy but we got together at my house and did the best we could. It was the first year that my mum and dad didn't host Christmas. For all our lives they had insisted on hosting it right up until the year before. They loved doing it, they made a really big occasion of it with tons of presents for all of us, now it was my turn.

Just after Dad died our dear friend Brenda died, she had been at dad's funeral. Brenda and Ged had spent many Christmases with our family over the years and it just seemed so cruel. Life can be so tough at times.

70

COLIN 80

Colin was due to turn 80 on August 19th 2018. After all the sadness I decided to plan a big surprise party for him.

I hired the Arun Yacht club in Littlehampton overlooking the river Arun and invited everyone to come.

He had a good turnout. Colin's family, mine, old friends like the Prior's from Primrose hill all of them including Dolly who had grown up with my dad. Old and new friends from Spain and all over the country came including friends from the Vauxhall and Brighton days and my oldest mate John Braine. I booked a fabulous cabaret singer Diane James and we really had a good "do" My Mum looked fantastic and she was proud to have my niece Sophie O'Connor and her first great grandchild 6 week old baby Freddie with her.

They had all generously clubbed together and paid for him (not me of course) to go on a Mediterranean cruise around the Greek islands, South of France, Italy, Malta and Spain. It was a fantastic trip and we both had the time of our lives.

Brother in law Brian O'connor

Colins family at his 80th

Deborah and mum on her 80th

dolly and mum nearly 90

family pic my 40th

Mum and dad brighton marina

Mum and Jonothan

My glamorous mum at 80

My lovley dad Don   Our newest family member Freddie

Sophie Freddie Mum abd Deborah

71

SO WHAT'S NEXT?

We bought a motor home to go traveling in. I christened it Pricilla Queen of the coast. Me being me saw a business opportunity as well as a holiday hobby. I set it up on websites and it wasn't long before bookings came in and I was back in the holiday rental game again. Renting out 'Pricilla' was successful straight away. There's a big market in motor home rental now. However after a few good lets somebody pranged it and then another family broke down in Cornwall and had to wait 8 hours for the breakdown team. I realised I was going through the same sort of worry and stress I had had with the house in Spain and thought to myself Oy that's it pack it up. Colin had never liked driving it and the beds were uncomfortable so we sold it. Luckily we didn't make a loss.

So instead we have just bought a 26.5 foot twin axle brand new caravan. A beauty. We are not going to rent it out it's just for us. We have just completed a caravan towing course. The plan is to tour the UK first in it. We have both travelled lots of places in the world but not seen much of Britain. Colin has had a few health issues lately and we are dealing with that but we are considering next winter to take the caravan down to Spain for 6 weeks if I can get things sorted out for mum.

Mums managing alright and she's still fiercely independent. She's still bright and smart, never moans, never complains, and does the Telegraph crossword everyday and loves watching rugby.

Until recently every time you went to visit she would always give you something, so you never left her house empty handed. It might be an Apple pie, a cake or just an apple or an orange in your hand but always something. Now she forgets but that's alright by us I'm incredibly proud of her.

72

I AM WHAT I AM

For me things are pretty good. I do miss Spain though for the winter, I get quite homesick even though I love England too. I miss the culture and the food and the bright blue skies, although I don't miss the house and the responsibility that went with it.

Maybe one day I'll end up back there to spend my old age sitting in the sun. It's certainly in my mind to do that and I always find a way so I'd put a bet on it.

I intend to grow old disgracefully. I'll be 60 next year and reckon I've got another 20 good years left to travel and explore. As I mentioned I don't party like I used to, the body can't cope with the hangovers anymore. Once you hit 50 it starts to say to you, please don't keep inflicting this on me. When I'm older and have no responsibilities I intend to resume my party lifestyle (a little bit anyway) I'll watch the sun go down with a large Vodka Martini and let someone else put me to bed, hopefully a handsome Spaniard.

On the other hand I get enormous pleasure walking by the sea with Lucca and growing things in my little but very nice garden. I read or play records on my vintage Hacker record player (I still have my records from my childhood) and I enjoy writing. After this book who knows?

Late nights out have lost their appeal unless it's to go for a nice meal or see a good show. I love my home and putting my feet up at night watching Netflix on a hugely vulgar 55 inch TV. I'm very political and enjoy huge rows and debates on Twitter. I'm an ardent Brexiteer. (Cue the groans)

Like everybody else I don't phone my friends enough and communicate through Facebook and what's app. whatever happens next I hope it won't be boring unless I want it to be. I don't think it will as I've still got the travel bug. I wonder who I'll meet on my caravan or cruising travels.

If the pension starts to get a bit thin maybe I'll do palm readings from the side of the road. Ideally if I can get away with it I'd like to pitch up in London for a few days. I've come a long way from where I was born; it would be great for a few nights to return. Park up on the top of Primrose hill and remember where I started. I might even take a wind up record player with me to play 'My mother's eyes' and Chubby Checker and annoy the neighbours like I used to do. I doubt if Jamie Oliver would approve now he lives opposite but that's never stopped me before.

Printed in Poland
by Amazon Fulfillment
Poland Sp. z o.o., Wrocław

49740630R00202